SPECIAL MESSAGE TO READERS

THE ULVERSCROFT FOUNDATION
(registered UK charity number 264873)

was established in 1972 to provide funds for research, diagnosis and treatment of eye diseases. Examples of major projects funded by the Ulverscroft Foundation are:-

- The Children's Eye Unit at Moorfields Eye Hospital, London
- The Ulverscroft Children's Eye Unit at Great Ormond Street Hospital for Sick Children
- Funding research into eye diseases and treatment at the Department of Ophthalmology, University of Leicester
- The Ulverscroft Vision Research Group, Institute of Child Health
- Twin operating theatres at the Western Ophthalmic Hospital, London
- The Chair of Ophthalmology at the Royal Australian College of Ophthalmologists

You can help further the work of the Foundation by making a donation or leaving a legacy. Every contribution is gratefully received. If you would like to help support the Foundation or require further information, please contact:

THE ULVERSCROFT FOUNDATION
The Green, Bradgate Road, Anstey
Leicester LE7 7FU, England
Tel: (0116) 236 4325

website: www.foundation.ulverscroft.com

THE PENGUIN LESSONS

Set against Argentina's turbulent years following the collapse of the corrupt Perónist regime, this is the story of Juan Salvador the penguin, rescued by English schoolteacher Tom Michell from an oil slick in Uruguay just days before a new term. When the bird refuses to leave Tom's side, the young teacher has no choice but to smuggle it across the border, through customs, and back to school. Whether it's as the rugby team's mascot, the housekeeper's confidant, the host at Tom's parties, or the most flamboyant swimming coach in world history, Juan Salvador transforms the lives of all he meets — in particular, one homesick schoolboy. As for Tom, he discovers in Juan Salvador a compadre like no other . . .

Blackpool Council

PAL

Please return/renew this item
by the last date shown.
Books may also be renewed by
phone or the Internet.

Tel: 01253 478070

www.blackpool.gov.uk

TOM MICHELL

THE PENGUIN LESSONS

Complete and Unabridged

CHARNWOOD
Leicester

First published in Great Britain in 2015 by
Michael Joseph
London

First Charnwood Edition
published 2016
by arrangement with
Michael Joseph
Penguin Random House
London

This book is based upon the author's memories and
recollection of events. However the names and identi-
fying characteristics of certain individuals have been
changed in order to protect their privacy, and dialogue,
characters and incidents have been reconstructed to
the the best of the author's recollection in order
to convey his story.

A catalogue record for this book is available
from the British Library.

ISBN 978–1–4448–2999–0

Published by
F. A. Thorpe (Publishing)
Anstey, Leicestershire

Set by Words & Graphics Ltd.
Anstey, Leicestershire
Printed and bound in Great Britain by
T. J. International Ltd., Padstow, Cornwall

This book is printed on acid-free paper

For W, A, M and C

Contents

Prologue......................................*1*

1. I Pick Up a Penguin 5
2. Magellan Penguins........................16
3. Bath Time 19
4. Storm Warning for the Falklands.........37
5. Strange Customs..........................48
6. You Shall Have a Fishy 69
7. Upstairs Downstairs 81
8. New Friends.............................96
9. Treasure Trove.........................102
10. Terrace Talk............................112
11. A Visit to the Zoo 118
12. The Mascot..............................133
13. A Visit to Maria's House 147
14. Going Wild for Penguins 158
15. The Quest for El Dorado 175
16. 'Can I Swim?' 193
17. And They All Lived Happily — 210
18. Reflections from Afar 219
    Epilogue.............................225
    Glossary of Spanish terms...........238
    Acknowledgements 240

South America

Venezuela
Colombia
Guyana
Suriname
French
Guiana
Atlantic
Ocean
Ecuador
Peru
Amazon
Andes
Brazil
Pacific
Ocean
Bolivia
Paraguay
Río Paraná
São Paulo
Chile
Uruguay
Buenos
Aires
Montevideo
Punta del Este
Río de la Plata
Argentina
Península Valdés
Patagonia
N
Tierra del Fuego

Prologue

Had I been told as a child in the 1950s that my life would one day run parallel with that of a penguin — that for a time, at least, it would be him and me against the world — I would have taken it in my stride. After all, my mother had kept three alligators at the house in Esher until they grew too big and too dangerous for that genteel town, when keepers from Chessington Zoo had come and removed them. She hadn't intended to keep alligators at the house in Esher. She had lived in Singapore until the age of sixteen and, on leaving to return to England, she had been given three eggs as a memento by her best friend in a tender and tearful farewell. The eggs had hatched, naturally, in her cabin during the long voyage and so, naturally, she had to take them home with her. Years later, in wistful moments, she sometimes remarked that the imaginative present was perhaps the most effective keepsake she had ever been given.

I knew wild and domestic animals well. My rural upbringing ensured I had a realistic view of life. I knew the fate of foxes and farm stock. However, exotic animals I knew only from zoos and my imagination. I, like Walt Disney Productions later, was inspired by the genius of Rudyard Kipling. I could identify completely with *The Jungle Book* and *Kim*, and his description of schooldays that were identical to my own more

1

than half a century later.

It's true. I was brought up with an Edwardian view of the world. My parents had been born in different parts of the Empire and I had grandparents, uncles, aunts and cousins scattered around the globe: Australia, New Zealand, Canada, South Africa, India, Ceylon (now Sri Lanka), Singapore, Rhodesia (Zimbabwe), Nyasaland (Malawi) and so on. To me, these places seemed almost familiar. Several times a year, letters — and, with rather less frequency, their authors — would arrive from those countries to fire my childish imagination with stories of 'Darkest Africa' and the like. But I wanted to explore somewhere different, uncharted territory, a real *Tierra Incognita*. South America was somewhere that nobody I knew appeared to have any experience of or connection with. So I had made up my mind while still at school that South America was where I would go when I grew up. At the age of twelve I bought a Spanish dictionary and secretly started learning Spanish phrases. When the opportunity arose, I'd be ready.

It was some ten years before that opportunity arrived, in the form of an advertisement in *The Times Educational Supplement*. 'Wanted,' it said, 'for HMC Boarding School in Argentina . . . ' The position was so clearly suited to my purpose that within half an hour my application was in the postbox and ready to wing its way across the Atlantic, announcing that they need look no further. As far as I was concerned, I was on my way.

I researched the economic and political situation before leaving, of course. An uncle in the Foreign Office gave me the inside track on

2

the fragility of the Perónist government in Argentina. There was likely to be another bloody coup by the army at some stage, our intelligence suggested. Terrorism was rife; murder and kidnappings were everyday events. Only the army could restore any order, it was thought. My bank in London, meanwhile, furnished me with economic information on Argentina: out-and-out wholesale mayhem! In short, everybody said, in an avuncular sort of way, that going to Argentina was an absurd notion and, under such circumstances, quite out of the question. Nobody in their right mind would dream of going. This, of course, was exactly what I wanted to hear and all the encouragement I needed.

I was offered the post of assistant master with residential responsibilities but the terms of my contract were not terribly promising. The college would pay for one return flight, conditional on my staying for a full academic year. My UK superannuation would be paid and I would be remunerated in local currency. What that would be worth in terms of buying power locally the headmaster couldn't say because of the prevailing economic shambles. However, I would be paid in accordance and commensurately with the other teaching staff. While I was resident in the college, food and lodging would be provided. That was it.

I made sure I had enough money in the bank to buy a return flight from Buenos Aires in the event of an emergency and my bank arranged with a branch of Banco de Londres y América del Sur in Buenos Aires that I could draw on funds in London should the need arise. But I didn't care about money. I was on my way, about to indulge that spirit of adventure I had felt as a boy; to embark on a quest to seek my destiny. That Fortune would assign me a penguin as a friend and fellow traveller, who would one day provide a wealth of bedtime stories for generations then unborn, was a singular twist of fate that still lay far over the western horizon.

Juan Salvador was a penguin who charmed and delighted everyone who knew him in those dark and dangerous days — days that saw the collapse of the Perónist government in terrorist outrages and violent revolution as Argentina teetered on the verge of anarchy. It was a time when liberties, opportunities and attitudes were so completely different from those of today. However, a young traveller like me and the inimitable, indomitable penguin, Juan Salvador, could — it turned out — be the happiest of companions after I rescued him in dramatic circumstances from deadly seas off the coast of Uruguay.

1

I Pick Up a Penguin

*In which one adventure ends and
another begins*

The seaside resort of Punta del Este can be found at that point on the coast of Uruguay where the great southerly sweep of South America's Atlantic seaboard meets the northern bank of the vast delta of the River Plate, or Río de la Plata. It lies some sixty miles to the east of the capital, Montevideo, and across the mighty river from Buenos Aires, the capital of the Republic of Argentina. In the 1960s and 1970s Punta del Este was, for the denizens of those two great metropolises, their Nice, Cannes or St Tropez; the place where the smart set went for summer holidays to escape the city heat, to stay and be seen in luxurious penthouses and apartment blocks facing the sea, and, for all I know, they do so still.

The key to one of those apartments had kindly been lent to me by the Bellamys, friends of mine who, because it was midwinter, were not using the apartment themselves. I was in Uruguay following an extraordinary stay in Paraguay and was making my way back to the Argentine via the gargantuan waterfalls at Iguazú, and then along the coast. After several weeks of exertions and excitements I was content to spend a few days relaxing in quiet, out-of-season Punta del Este.

I had returned to the apartment late in the afternoon on my last day in order to pack and organize my belongings ready for a very early departure the following morning. My booking for the hydrofoil across the River Plate was for twelve noon, which required that I catch the *colectivo*, the local bus, from Punta del Este to Montevideo at a quarter to six in the morning. *Colectivos* were enthusiastically decorated by their drivers with innumerable diverse adornments and good-luck charms, which were supposed to make up for the bald tyres, I think.

Having packed, cleaned and checked the apartment, I decided to take a final walk by the sea before going out for what would be my last supper at the resort.

The harbour at Punta del Este, on the western side of the point, was small, sufficient only for a few score fishing boats and pleasure craft, which on that day were rocking gently on their moorings, in harmony with the floating pontoons along which owners could walk to reach their dinghies. Although the harbour is well defended against the Atlantic Ocean to the east, there was little protection from the westerly breeze that was blowing that day.

The air was full of the cry of gulls, the slap of halyards and the smell of fish, and this little haven of security basked serenely in the bright winter sunlight. The vibrant colours of the gulls, boats and houses were shown to their best advantage against the sapphire sea and azure sky. My attention, however, was drawn towards the countless thousands of fish in the cold, crystal-clear water. Swimming in unison, shoals of sprats raced around the harbour, attempting to evade their predators by zigzagging or by dividing and reuniting every few seconds. I was mesmerized by the scintillating waves of light that pulsed across the water like an aurora as the sun reflected off the iridescent bodies of the fish.

Next to the rusting, antiquated fuel pumps marked in gallons, and housed under a corrugated iron roof, a muscle-bound fisher-woman scooped her living from the harbour with a large green net, securely tied to a stout bamboo pole. She wore a leather apron, rubber boots and a satisfied expression although, I noted, she had bare hands. Her hair was covered with a brown scarf and her face was deeply lined and weathered. Beside her were three wooden casks, filled almost to the brim with sprats, which I presumed accounted for her satisfaction. Standing ankle-deep in flapping silver-banded fish, she dropped her net into the water and lifted a fresh catch almost every minute, to the dismay of the gulls who scolded her noisily. She gave a toothless grin as she shook each new haul into the barrels and picked out the few fish that hadn't fallen from the net, something I realized she couldn't have done wearing gloves. The little black-backed, swallow-tailed gulls, after hovering briefly about ten feet above the sea, dived down then bobbed up to the surface to sit on the water with sprats glistening like rubber mercury in their beaks. In another flash, the catch was swallowed.

There were a couple of penguins in the harbour, too, enjoying their share. It was captivating to watch them fly so fast through the water in pursuit of the fish, far more skilfully even than the gulls in the air. Twisting and turning, they tore through the shoals with breathtaking speed and agility, snapping up sprats as the fish scattered before them. Against such a superlative adversary the sprats appeared to be almost defenceless, other perhaps than their seemingly limitless numbers. I was only surprised that there weren't more penguins there to feast on such rich and easy pickings.

I could gladly have watched them for much longer, but as the penguins swam out of view, I turned and walked round the promontory to the eastern side and so on to the next breakwater. Small, white-flecked waves were rolling in from the ocean and breaking on the beach. I had only been strolling along the seashore for ten, maybe fifteen, minutes on that beautiful afternoon, reflecting on all my new experiences, the wonderful and awe-inspiring things I had seen and done on holiday, when I caught sight of the first of them: black, unmoving shapes. Initially, I was aware of only a few but, as I walked on, they grew in number, until the whole beach appeared to be covered with black lumps in a black carpet. Hundreds of oil-drenched penguins lay dead in the sand, from the high-water mark to the sea and stretching far away along the shore to the north. Dead penguins, covered in thick, cloying, suffocating oil and tar. The sight was so dreadful, so sickening and depressing, that I could only wonder what future lay ahead for any 'civilization' that could tolerate, let alone perpetrate, such desecration. I understood then why there were so few penguins in the harbour catching sprats, despite the abundance of the fish. Evidently, only a lucky few had avoided the oil slick.

Consumed by dark thoughts, I continued my walk above the trail of devastation that covered much of the beach, trying to estimate the number of dead birds. Even if I had been able to calculate how many penguins were on the shore — in places heaped on top of each other — it was impossible to assess the number of bodies churning in the sea. Each wave that broke piled more birds on top of those already there, while further out every new breaker was sweeping another grim batch of black carcasses towards the shore.

The beach between the sea and the wall at the side of the road was narrow, possibly only thirty yards at its widest, but the pollution along the beach extended as far as I could see. Clearly, thousands of penguins had died in the most horrifying manner while they were making their way north along their ancestral migration routes just as their forebears had done for millions of years.

I still don't know why I continued to walk along the beach that day. Possibly I needed to understand just how appalling this event was

— the extent of the damage. I hadn't heard any reports of an oil spill in this part of the world but in those days regulations regarding the conduct of oil tankers were less stringent and compliance minimal, so occurrences like this were not uncommon. After discharging cargo at their destinations, oil tankers would put to sea again and wash out their tanks while in transit to collect a new consignment.

It was events such as these that eventually provoked much-needed change. I had little doubt that what I was witnessing on this beach was the inevitable consequence of a hideous collision of cultures. When the instinctive, annual compulsion of seabirds to migrate met a vast, floating oil slick dumped at sea through human thoughtlessness and greed, there was only one possible outcome: the utter and complete annihilation of those penguins. This would have been indescribably ghastly had it been the result of an accident. That it should be the result of deliberate actions taken in the full knowledge of the likely consequences defied any kind of rationalization or acceptance.

I had been walking briskly, unwilling to focus too closely on the details of the dead creatures, when, out of the corner of my eye, I thought I saw a movement. Not from the churning spume of the surf, but from the stillness on the beach. I stopped and watched. I hadn't been mistaken. One valiant bird was alive; a single surviving soul struggling amid all that death. It was extraordinary! How could one solitary bird still be living when the oil and tar had so comprehensively overwhelmed the rest?

Although it was lying on its belly and covered in tar like the other birds, this penguin was moving its wings and holding its head up. It wasn't moving much, but its head and wings were giving little spasmodic jerks. The death throes of a defeated creature, I assumed.

I watched for a short time. Could I walk on and abandon it to the poisonous oil and the exhausting, suffocating tar that would slowly extinguish its life? I decided that I could not; I had to end its suffering as quickly as possible. So I headed towards it, clearing space under each footstep with as much decency and respect for the dead birds as was possible.

I had no clear plan of how I was going to administer the *coup de grâce*. In fact, I had no plan at all. But as that solitary penguin, indistinguishable from the thousands of other tar-dripping penguins in all but one respect — this one was alive — struggled to its feet to face yet another adversary, all thoughts of such violence vanished from my mind. Flapping sticky wings at me and with a darting raptor beak, it stood its ground ready to fight for its life once more. It was almost knee high!

I checked my advance and looked again at this penguin's companions. Was I wrong? Were they alive after all? Perhaps just resting, recovering? I turned a few bodies over with my toe. No spark of life appeared in any bird apart from this one, nothing to distinguish one dead penguin from the next. Their plumage and throats were choked up with tar, hideously deformed tongues were protruding from their beaks and their eyes were

11

completely covered with the corrosive filth. The stink of bitumen alone would have overcome the birds and I wouldn't have been walking along the beach myself had not the wind been blowing from the west, carrying the stench out to sea.

Amid all this obscenity there was just this single penguin with an open, red-tongued beak and clear eyes, jet black and sparking with anger. I suddenly felt a surge of hope kindling for this exception. Could it survive if cleaned? I had to give it a chance, surely? But how would I approach this filthy and aggressive bird? We stood there, eyeing each other suspiciously, evaluating our respective opponents.

Quickly, I scanned the accumulated rubbish along the beach: bits of wood, plastic bottles, crumbling polystyrene, disintegrating fishing net, all the familiar things found along the high-water mark on almost every beach tainted by our advanced society. I also had a bag containing an apple in my pocket. As I moved away, the penguin settled back down on its tummy and shook its bottom as though getting comfortable again. Hurriedly, I gathered some of the flotsam and jetsam that I thought might be of assistance. Now, gladiator-like, I approached my quarry which, sensing the renewed threat, immediately reared up to its full height. Swirling a piece of fishing net, I distracted the penguin and, with the swiftness and bravery of Achilles, dropped the net over its head and pushed it over with a stick. I pinned it down and, with my hand inside the bag (it was no time to be eating apples), grabbed its feet.

12

I lifted the furious creature, twisting and turning in its efforts to escape, clear of the beach and away from my body and discovered for the first time how heavy penguins could be.

And so back to the Bellamys' apartment with a flapping ten-pound bird. If my arm were to tire and that vicious beak come within striking distance, it would skewer my leg and smear me with tar. I was apprehensive about hurting it or scaring it to death and I was trying to ensure it didn't suffer at my hands, but I was also concerned about my own well-being during the return journey of a mile or more.

My mind teemed with half-formed plans as I made the return journey. What was I going to say to anyone who challenged me? Was I allowed to pick up tar-soaked penguins in Uruguay? Most countries in South America at that time were police states and I wouldn't have been surprised had there been some absurd law forbidding such a rescue.

At least I should be able to clean the penguin, I decided, as I jogged unevenly back along the beach road. I remembered we had used butter to remove tar from beach towels when we were children, and I knew I had some butter in the fridge in the flat, as well as olive oil, margarine and detergent.

Carrying the bird at arm's length was exhausting work and I had to change hands frequently. I was holding it by its feet but, fearful of causing any further injury to the frantic creature, I kept a finger between its legs in order to gauge the strength of my grip. I was under no illusion; this was not comfortable for the bird. However, we eventually reached our destination without major mishap to either of us. Despite its best endeavours, the penguin had failed to wound me — and I hadn't been tempted to finish it off en route.

My next problem was how to slip by the fearsome concierge, who occupied an office under the stairs. Throughout my stay she had come rushing out, like a savage guard dog, to scrutinize every visitor as they came and went, as though we weren't to be trusted. It was abundantly clear why the building management had engaged the services of this particular individual to ensure that visitors behaved respectably during their stay, so naturally suited was she to the task. But by some curious twist of fate, on the one occasion she might have had real cause for concern, she wasn't there. The coast was clear.

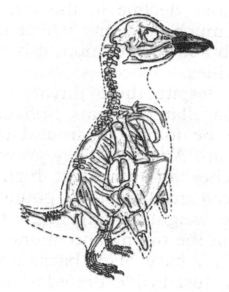

'a little about penguins is revealed'

2

Magellan Penguins

In which a little about penguins is revealed

The populations of penguin colonies have suffered serious decline in the last forty years, some by as much as eighty per cent and more. This is attributed to pollution, fishing and other human activities.

However, despite these threats to their very existence, Magellan penguins, *Spheniscus magellanicus*, can be found all around the southern coasts of South America. They grow to between eighteen inches and two feet high and weigh between seven and fourteen pounds, although their precise weight at any given time is very dependent on the timing and abundance of their last meal. They have black backs and faces and white fronts. Just inside the edge of their white fronts there is a decorative black inverted 'U'.

Out of the water they are not graceful birds. They appear to have long bodies and short legs. Their shoulders, or scapulas, are set low on their bodies and the bones of their wings are astonishingly flat and thin, giving them the profile of a boomerang. A penguin's natural stance is with bent knees and an 'S'-shaped neck, but they can change their shape to a remarkable degree. When they squat, they become almost round, which helps with heat conservation, but they can also stand up straight, where upon they appear very slim, tall and elegant.

When standing erect, they spread their webbed toes wide so their 'heels' are then above their toes, but they can 'sit', with their heels and their bottoms touching the ground. This triangular contact with the ground is a very stable arrangement. When seated on a low stool human leg bones are placed in a similar way, but penguins have more tail bones than we do, which they can sit on. Most of their leg bones are hidden within their body, which comes down almost to their heels (one of the main reasons penguins don't get cold legs!). The overall effect is of two extremely stubby legs protruding below their abdomens. The geometry of their bones makes them very pigeon-toed so, when walking, they waddle with a rolling, rotating gait, comical to watch.

Magellan penguins are monogamous, mating for life. While nesting, parent birds each take turns of ten to fifteen days to incubate the eggs, one fasting while the other feeds. When penguins are young, the scales and skin of their feet and legs are blotchy, but these become darker as they age. The penguin I had found had no light blotches so he was a mature bird.

In the water, penguins are transformed. When swimming on the surface a penguin resembles a rather deflated duck, with only head and tail above water, but below the waves they are simply sublime. No cheetah, stallion, albatross or condor is more elegant or graceful. Nothing is more masterful in the water.

17

Of course, I knew absolutely nothing about penguins the day I picked one up on Punta del Este beach, but that deplorable state of ignorance was about to come to an abrupt end.

3

Bath Time

*In which more than one of us has a bath
we didn't want and a seagull comes to the rescue*

As I entered the flat and looked around I realized
that I had been carried away with the idea of
rescuing the penguin and had not given a thought
to the practicalities that cleaning one would involve.
The Bellamys' flat was elegant and tasteful. It
looked like an advertisement from a glossy maga-
zine — the last place to bring an oil-soaked
penguin. The possibility of doing anything that
might benefit the bird now began to seem very
remote while the chances of making a real mess
in the flat, upsetting the Bellamys by spoiling
their décor, and getting myself injured into the
bargain, all seemed very real. The penguin was
filthy and very aggressive. Its beak snapped shut
with a metallic clack like a pair of dental pliers as
it continually twisted and turned in its attempts
to savage me.

For a moment I was tempted to take the bird
back to the beach rather than start on a fool-
hardy course of action that I would likely regret.
How could I contain and clean this struggling
creature against its will, without damaging it
further or wrecking the flat? Then I had an idea.

I had with me a string bag, an old faithful,

19

which I always travelled with because it was so useful. It was like a large version of the nets that oranges are sold in, except that mine was blue and had drawstring handles. I had kept it since my schooldays when we used them for carrying rugby boots and balls, because the mud would simply drop through the holes. Woven into a net of small squares, it was ideal for taking on adventures; it occupied almost no space but was robust enough to carry almost any impulsive acquisition during an expedition, as it was about to demonstrate so admirably now. One-handed, I shook it out and dropped the bird inside before slipping a broomstick through the handles and suspending the bag between the backs of two chairs I had arranged for the purpose. Deftly, I placed newspaper — a copy of *El Día* — on the floor between the chairs and under the bird and, satisfied that I had contained the creature, I set about searching the flat for suitable cleaning agents.

I collected butter and margarine, olive oil and cooking oil, soap, shampoo and detergent, and arranged them in the bathroom. This room, like the rest of the flat, was furnished with taste and deep pockets. Pretty tessellated tiles — salmon pink and fish-shaped — covered the walls, and the floor was a polished black marble. The units themselves were made from ivory-coloured porcelain with gold fittings — I couldn't dream up a more unsuitable place for cleaning a tar-sodden penguin.

After filling the bidet with warm water, I lifted the bag from its temporary support, with the bird still safely inside, and placed it in the bowl. The increasingly irate creature had been struggling and its feet and beak were now protruding, allowing it the opportunity to clamp one of my fingers in its powerful bill. First blood to the bird! I cursed it as I tried to extract my finger but, terrier-like, it wasn't letting go without a fight. I couldn't believe how hard it could bite; it could have opened a tin of beans with that beak.

'*Damn you! Let go!*' I yelled as I held its head as gently as my pain and fury would allow and prised its beak open. It had inflicted a deep and painful cut that was bleeding profusely and hurt as much as if I had jammed it in a heavy door. I was astonished that a mere bird could do that amount of damage and examined it in amazement. Leaving the bird in the bidet, entangled in the bag, I attended to my finger. Holding it under cold running water, I could barely believe the extent of the cut; I still carry the scar to this day. I let it bleed into the basin and cursed myself for not leaving the bird where I had found it.

I glowered at the penguin and the penguin stared straight back at me. Unflinching and belligerent, its black, malevolent eyes said it all. They shone with pure loathing and venom:

'*Come on then, you great brute! There is more where that came from!*' they said.

'*Damn you, you stupid . . . stupid bird!*' I replied. '*I'm trying to help you! Can't you even understand that, birdbrain?*'

I wrapped my finger in loo paper in a futile attempt to stop the bleeding, continually replacing it as the paper became sodden, and held my hand above my head. My finger was throbbing. What vile diseases did penguins carry, I wondered? After some fifteen minutes I had managed to stem the flow of gore with a gauze bandage and sticking plasters and was reluctantly ready to return to the fray.

It was clear that I was going to have to control the creature far more effectively than I had done so far. I had made the mistake of underestimating my opponent, thinking it was just a little bird when, in fact, it was every bit as big and dangerous as a golden eagle defending its eyrie. I had to immobilize it properly this time. Snatching the bag up by the handles, so it was unable to savage me with either its beak or feet, I suspended the bird between the chairs again and with some of the bandage I prepared a loop which I slipped round its feet and pulled tight as its beak snapped repeatedly on thin air. Penguins have enormous and extremely strong feet, which are equipped with very sharp talons not unlike those of an eagle, and can shred human skin. Interestingly, the undersides of penguins' feet are not a bit bird-like but are more like a monkey's: fleshy, muscular and dexterous. I bound its feet from the back, where its beak couldn't reach me.

While the penguin flapped and floundered ineffectually in the bag, I held its head firmly with newspaper and brute force. Using some stout rubber bands that I had found during my search for cleaning equipment, I encircled its beak several times, carefully avoiding its nostrils, and I terminated the last loop by placing a final twist of rubber across its sharp point. Its feet scrabbled at the air as it tried to twist and turn but, hanging in the bag, it couldn't reach me. It was breathing hard and its pulse was visibly throbbing in its throat and head as it continued to kick and struggle, all to no avail, since it was unable to get a purchase on anything.

Its eyes, normally the size of peas, bulged with fury, frustration and hatred.

'*How dare you! I'll make you pay for this! You see if I don't!*' they said. It was hard to believe that the penguin had been at death's door only a short time ago. There was nothing for it but to adopt the clinical detachment of a vet. The bird wouldn't survive unless I cleaned it properly.

'*Right then, you bloody little bird,*' I said. '*Come here! I've got to be cruel to be kind!*' My finger throbbed and hurt and any sympathy I might have felt for the penguin had all but gone down the drain with my blood. Making sure its feet were securely trussed, I tied the handles of the bag around its body to hold its wings close.

Satisfied that it was finally subdued, I put it back in the bidet and began the cleaning process by pouring a handful of washing-up liquid over its back. Now that its beak was no longer a dangerous weapon, I was able to work the detergent into its short, stubby feathers. The task was not made any easier by the dressing on my wounded finger or by the wriggling of the bird, but the string bag worked perfectly as a restraint, holding it gently without restricting the cleaning.

Suddenly, the exhausted penguin lay still. The change in attitude and behaviour was astonishingly rapid, far faster than I can now relate.

Within moments of being a terrified, hostile and resentful animal (which was, quite understandably, determined to exact revenge on me, a representative of the race that had so cruelly exterminated thousands of its closest relatives), it became a docile and cooperative partner in this clean-up operation. The transformation occurred as I washed off the first of the detergent. It were as if the bird had suddenly understood that I was trying to rid it of that disgusting oil rather than commit murder. I drained the bidet and refilled it with warm water. The penguin's eyes no longer bulged like goldfish bowls. It had ceased shaking its head, trying to flap its wings or inflict damage on me with its beak and feet, but was watching calmly as the water flowed. Its pulse had stopped racing and it no longer looked defiantly straight at me like an aggrieved captive. It was turning its head from side to side, regarding me quizzically with each eye in turn. Penguins are hunters and can look straight ahead with binocular vision but they have the avian habit of looking first with one eye and then with the other.

'*What's your game then? Why are you doing this? Do you know how to clean off this foul muck?*' the eyes asked.

On the second dose of detergent it didn't shrink away. Sensing our relationship was changing, I decided to risk releasing him from the bag, which allowed me to rub the green solvent into the feathers of his back and wings more easily. He held his wings out helpfully so that no part should be missed as the detergent did its work. I rubbed the washing-up liquid all over the penguin's feathers and then scraped off the resulting gooey mixture. After each wash he shook himself like a dog to dry.

Because he had become so cooperative, I removed the elastic band from his beak and untied his feet, which made the cleaning process so very much easier. He made no attempt to peck me or to escape, but his head bobbed about constantly as, with obvious curiosity, he watched my hands working the detergent into his feathers. Looking first with one eye and then the other, he made careful note of the progress being achieved and continually looked at my face to check that I was paying proper attention to the delicate task I was undertaking.

When the washing-up liquid was finished, I started with the shampoo and so I was able to wash every bit of the bird several times. Standing upright in the bidet, he allowed me to do my work with no resistance at all. Neither did he try to remove any of the soapy, tarry emulsion with his beak, nor make any objection as I carefully cleaned around his face and eyes, which I did with butter alone.

At the end of an hour's work, I had a recognizable penguin. His back feathers were black again, if not sleek and shiny, and his tummy feathers, though not pristine, were at least a greyish sort of white. I let the water out of the bidet for the last time and, when I didn't refill it, the penguin studied me closely. We regarded each other for some moments as I looked directly at the result of my handiwork.

'Is that it? Have you finished? Are we done? I hope you haven't missed any!'

Slowly, my focus moved beyond the bird and out around the bathroom. His shaking after each wash had deposited a thin film of dirty detergent, oil and water over a fair proportion of the walls and, I saw as I looked in the mirror, over me too.

Although he was now clean to the touch, I didn't want him wandering free in the flat so, in order to constrain him, I placed him in the bath while I started to clean both the bathroom and myself. He appeared to be exhausted and lay on his tummy, with occasional shakes of his bottom, watching me while I took a shower and washed the splatterings from my face and hair.

The average penthouse holiday flat is rarely equipped with the necessities for de-tarring penguins and the Bellamys' was certainly no exception, so I made a quick trip to the local market, where I bought large quantities of paper towels and replaced the washing-up liquid. I also bought a tin of sardines, the only thing I could find which I thought the penguin might want for his tea. As I shopped, I trawled the recesses of my brain for scraps of whatever knowledge I might have gleaned at some time or another about the Natural History of Penguins because I was just beginning to have a few doubts. A little voice was nagging at me, suggesting that washing seabirds with detergent might remove their natural waterproofing, preventing them from coping in their element; that they would become waterlogged, sink and drown. If that were true, then I'd just done an excellent job of removing every bit of waterproofing from that penguin.

After everything we'd been through, I was extremely conscious of his well-being. I was trying to help him, after all, but with no instant access to information on the subject of cleaning sea-birds — no opportunity in those days to Google 'how to de-tar a penguin' — I had to rely on memory and common sense.

Walking back to the flat through the deserted streets, the reality of my own situation was also dawning on me, casting a shadow over our progress so far. I had to be up at dawn to begin my journey home to Buenos Aires and there I would have to prepare to go back to work; all of this was arranged and immutable. How could I possibly cope with a disabled penguin in tow? Obviously, I didn't want to keep the penguin. It just wouldn't be possible to keep a penguin in a flat in Buenos Aires. I needed a penguin like a penguin needs a motorbike. As it happened, a motorbike was my means of transport in Argentina. Unfortunately, with legs like theirs, penguins can't ride pillion!

I reasoned with myself that I had no real evidence about the washing of pelagic birds and it was probably just an old wives' tale anyway. Determinedly, I retraced my steps and prepared to release the penguin back into the sea, so that I could get on with all the important things I had to do in readiness for the start of term. There was simply no question about it, he would just have to return to the ocean and take his chances. I couldn't keep a penguin and he'd be better off with his own kind.

I had left him in the bath and on my return to the bathroom he ran up and down in the tub, flapping his wings. His little eyes were sparkling.

'*You've been a long time!*' they said. '*I was wondering what had happened to you. What have you been doing?*'

Had he been a dog he would have been wagging his tail and I was convinced he was pleased to see me.

I opened the tin of sardines with the attached key and tried offering him pieces of fish. His reaction was disdainful. I tried putting little bits on his beak, but he vehemently shook them off. When I offered him more, he tucked his beak down on to his chest and his multiple eyelids closed, then opened again to look at me.

'*Here, I've brought you some sardines for your tea,*' I said.

'*Yuck, yuck, yuck! Take it away! What is that filth?*'

I gave up, dried him off with the paper towels and set about making him waterproof again by rubbing butter and olive oil into his feathers until he resembled a greased-up swimmer. Once I was satisfied he was saturated with all the waterproofing materials available to me, I put the penguin in a shopping bag to hide him from the harridan thinly disguised as a concierge. Together, we quietly headed back out to the sea.

Only the coast road separated the Bellamys' apartment from the Atlantic. The beach here was pleasantly sandy with rocky outcrops; there was no sign of the oil spill, nor of the ill-fated penguins which had blanketed the shore stretching away to the north-east of the point.

Crossing the road rapidly, I walked down to

the water's edge, placed him on the wet sand and stepped back to watch. I expected him to rush into the sea and swim away, happy to be free once more. But he didn't. He walked straight back to my side. Worse still, he was looking at my face, directly into my eyes even, and appeared to be talking to me.

'Why are you trying to send me back to that deadly oily ocean so soon after we've met and become friends?'

'Go on,' I said, 'go and find your fellow penguins. You can't come with me!'

But instead he just stood at my feet, looking at me pathetically.

'I can't go back! I can't swim now you've washed out my water-proofing.'

Oh, hell! This was not going according to plan, not at all. I picked him up and carried him out on to the rocks.

'You can't come with me,' I explained patiently. 'I'm going back to Argentina tomorrow. I have to work on Monday. You just can't come with me. You've got to swim off now.'

A slight swell coming in from the Atlantic was making the water rise and fall by a couple of feet. I waited for a trough, placed him on the rocks and skipped back on to a higher point. Within seconds the next wave came in and he disappeared from view. I waited, straining my eyes in an attempt to catch sight of him swimming off through the water. But, after a few moments, the sea receded again and he was gone. I must have missed him amid the reflections from the surface.

29

'*Goodbye, little bird,*' I said. '*Good luck. Henceforth, may your path be untrammelled and untroubled!*' But as I turned to go, there again, struggling out of the water, was a bedraggled penguin. He must have swum round in a circle and failed to find his way out into the open sea. I would just have to try again and place him further out, at the end of the rocks where his way would be clear.

I studied the rocks that could be seen above the water and the frequency of the waves as they came in. The rise and fall of the waves had a period of several seconds between crests. Confident I could get further out to sea, I picked the bird up and waited. Split-second timing was essential.

It was already getting dark and the sea was very cold. I set off across the rocks as the water fell. Counting seconds in my mind, I placed the penguin at the furthest point I thought I could reach and started back. Before I had got halfway, however, I saw I was going to get wet feet. As my stepping stones disappeared under the foam, I missed my footing and found myself stumbling up to my knees in freezing water. 'Hell!' I gasped as a cold sea wave surged around me, soaking me to the waist. Struggling on, I made my way to the beach, but not before I slipped again, plunging my arm into the sea up to my shoulder in order to save myself from total immersion and skinning my palm in the process.

'Typical! When will you learn to leave well alone?' I asked myself.

I stood on the beach feeling the chill as the

wind rose and caused my wet clothes to flap. I looked down at my soaking shoes, my jeans sticking to my legs. I felt the arm of my jacket cling to me as the water drained down my sleeve, streaming from the cuff, and I watched as it cascaded on to the sand below. That was when I became conscious of a pair of feet standing next to mine.

I raised my eyes and realized I was being studied in my discomfort.

'*Water's cold, isn't it?*'

'*Look! I'm soaking wet thanks to you!*' I said to the penguin who was now standing beside me, looking me up and down.

'*And your waterproofing doesn't work either, does it?*' he implied.

I demanded that he get back to his own kind and, walking rapidly back up the beach with water squirting from my shoes, I hoped sincerely that the concierge would still be away. Preventing visitors from trailing seaweed and sand through the building was exactly what she was paid to do.

The retaining wall at the edge of the road was about three feet above the beach and, although there were no steps at that point, an outcrop of rocks provided me with a convenient exit.

What exactly did I feel as I looked back and saw that the bird was now running up the beach after me? I was too wet and cold and the salt water was stinging the cuts on my hand too much for me to feel pleased by the persistence of the penguin. However, the sea wall was too high for him to scale so once he understood that he couldn't follow me I was sure he'd have no

31

option but to find his own way back to the sea. I would have to force myself to adopt the impartiality of wildlife photographers and resist interfering further — there was simply nothing more I could do for him.

Pausing only to allow a car to pass, I crossed the road and turned towards my apartment block. I glanced back. There, on the opposite side, was a penguin scaling the rocks and walking towards me.

'*Stop!*' I yelled, at both the penguin and a speeding van as it hurtled down the road towards us, but the driver didn't hear me or see the penguin. I dreaded a bump as it passed. None came. Once the vehicle had gone by, there was the bird, walking across the road. Without wasting another second, I rushed over and picked him up. He was soaking wet and felt very cold.

'*What am I going to do with you?*' I asked.

I was reprimanded by that nagging voice in my head again: 'I told you, seabirds can't survive in the water if you wash them with detergent!' Why did it sound so like my mother?

Carefully, I put him into the bag, folded the top over and, holding him against my chest for warmth, walked through the glass doors into the building.

'Oh! Señor, whatever has happened to you? Are you all right?' asked the concierge, who seemed genuinely concerned as she came out from behind her desk, looking at my wet clothes and the blood dripping to the floor from my hand.

'I'm afraid I slipped by the sea and fell in. I'm fine, really, no bones broken. I just need to have a hot shower before I catch my death of cold.'

'Did you fall from the rocks? They are slippery. Are you sure you didn't hurt yourself badly?'

'No, I'm fine, thank you, really! Absolutely fine. I just need to change,' I said as I manoeuvred round her. My shoes squelched and left sandy puddles where I stepped. I was anxious to get away quickly before she came fussing around me and discovered the penguin. 'Oh, I'm sorry about the mess! I'll clean it all up just as soon as I've changed.' Without waiting for a reply, I rushed up the stairs.

'Leave it to me, señor,' she called after me. 'You go and have a hot shower!' Of course, it was a different concierge on duty. Perhaps not all the fates were against me.

Back in the flat, I returned the penguin to the bath and dried him off once again with paper towels, took a quick shower and put my things on the radiators to dry. Then I busied myself trying to remove any shred of evidence that might betray the fact I had allowed a penguin into the Bellamys' bathroom, a task which took just as long as the cleaning of the bird. When all was done, I checked my packing, the hydrofoil reservation and timetable, and began to think about dinner. I'd eaten everything in the fridge but the apple and the penguin's sardines, neither of which seemed adequate for the last night of my holiday. I had planned to eat out, but that was before I had a penguin to look after. Making sure he was thoroughly dry, I returned the bird to the bath, for there was nothing more I could do for him. I picked up my book and decided it would be safe to go out for dinner.

I was reluctantly coming to the conclusion that I would have to try to take him back to Argentina with me. My timetable was too tight to allow me to look for a zoo in Montevideo and deposit him there and, besides, if I took him to the zoo in Buenos Aires I'd be able to see him from time to time. Relieved that I had hit upon a sensible solution to the problem, I set out with my mind at ease.

There was an atmospheric little restaurant a few hundred yards from the flat and I decided to go there for my last meal in Uruguay. I ordered some olives to be followed by the usual steak and chips with salad, and a bottle of my favourite health-promoting Argentine Malbec from the glorious province of Mendoza to wash it all down.

It was still early and with no other diners to talk to I finally relaxed and opened my book. *Jonathan Livingston Seagull* was a very popular novella in the early 1970s and I had been reading the Spanish edition, *Juan Salvador Gaviota*. But, despite my best efforts, I found I could not focus my attention on seagulls at all. I was thinking about a certain penguin in a bath. In all probability he would be dead when I got back. It was a certainty, I thought. The wretched creature must have swallowed significant quantities of oil and would soon die of poisoning. It was inevitable. It just didn't seem possible that one and only one penguin should be able to live through the toxins and trauma that had killed every other bird on that beach. He would be dead in the bath when I got back, I concluded, and all I had done was make his final hours more miserable. I kept looking at the book, but the words just danced on the page in front of me: *Juan Salvador, Juan Salvador . . .*

All of a sudden I found I was hoping against hope that the penguin would survive because, as of that instant, he had a name and his name was Juan Salvador Pingüino, and with his name came a surge of hope and the beginning of a bond that would last a lifetime. That was the moment at which he became my penguin, and whatever the future held, we'd face it together.

I ate my meal with undue haste, settled the bill and raced back to the flat, anticipating the worst. But on opening the front door I knew all was well because I could hear him running up and down in the bath and flapping his wings in welcome. As I entered the bathroom he looked at me in his inimitable way:

'*I'm so glad you're back! You've been an awfully long time,*' he seemed to be saying and I found I was smiling at him — or, rather more precisely, I was grinning from ear to ear, relief flooding through me.

'*Yes, Juan Salvador, I'm back, and I'm so glad to see you looking so well!*'

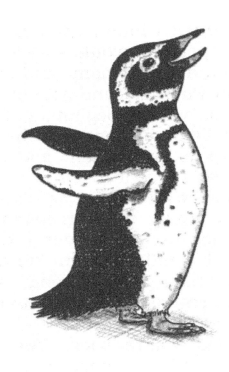

'Yes, Juan Salvador, I'm back, and I'm so glad to
see you looking so well!'

4

Storm Warning for the Falklands

In which a bar brawl leads to a plan

I went to bed that night trying to devise a plan for getting a penguin into Argentina, through customs and over the border, without being stopped. I was going to rely on my understanding of the national psyche of the country, of which I had acquired considerable knowledge even though I had been living in Argentina for just six months. Following my experiences in my first week living in Quilmes, a suburb of Buenos Aires, I considered myself an expert on the subject and I owed much of that knowledge to my new colleague, a history teacher by the name of Euan McCree.

St George's College is a boarding school modelled on English public schools, its original buildings constructed in a splendid colonial style, and in some ways it had got stuck in the 1920s. It had been founded in 1898 by one Canon Stevenson for the education of the children of the British who lived and worked in Argentina, principally involved in building railways, refrigerated packing stations and ranching, and for whom the cost in both time and money to educate their children in England was prohibitive. But by the 1970s its clientele had changed. Although many of its pupils were still of British extraction (in many cases fathers and grand-fathers had attended the college), they were by then second- or third-generation Argentine and no longer considered England 'home'. The majority, however, came from Argentine families of Hispanic descent.

St George's is the only boarding school in Argentina that is a member of the Headmasters' Conference or HMC schools. As such it is extremely exclusive and expensive and at that time considered itself the very pinnacle of secondary education in South America, attracting pupils from most of the other countries on that continent. Most lessons were given in Spanish, the Argentine National Curriculum was followed and pupils were taught by locally qualified staff, which was appropriate for students who expected to continue their education and make their living in that country. Only some twenty per cent followed an exclusively English curriculum of O and A levels and a number of British staff were engaged to teach those subjects and maintain the standard of spoken English expected by fee-paying parents.

I had met Euan on my journey to Argentina from England. We were the two new members of staff that year. About five years my senior, he was six foot three, with unruly, though not long, dark brown hair and beard, which contrasted with his fair skin. In fact, he was the spitting image of Captain Haddock of *Tintin* fame, but looks were where the likeness ended. Euan possessed one of the most formidable intellects I have ever encountered. His knowledge on almost every topic was simply encyclopaedic. This appeared more remarkable because he had been brought up in the very toughest part of Belfast, Northern Ireland, or Ulster as he referred to it. His father had been a shop steward in the Harland and Wolff shipyards. His accent was the broadest imaginable and, on first meeting, he was very difficult for an Englishman to understand because of his dialect.

Euan had an astounding, preternatural memory and could quote great chunks of poetry or literature after a single reading. He was never other than intense. He wanted to discuss Nietzsche at breakfast and, if one wasn't very vigilant in responding, it was quite possible to be wrong-footed and trapped into appearing sympathetic to some wholly abhorrent position like compulsory euthanasia. Eventually, I found it better simply to pretend to be totally absorbed in something utterly compelling in the newspapers, something that required my *undivided* attention, like the Report of Shipping Movements in the Port of Buenos Aires. But all that I discovered on better acquaintance.

So it was during our first days living in Argentina, as our confidence slowly increased, we had decided we needed to broaden our knowledge further by visiting the centre of Buenos Aires to sample some of the nightlife. Accordingly, we had taken the train from Quilmes station to the city centre terminal at Constitución, then the *subte* — the underground; an abbreviation of *subterráneo* — to the central Avenue 9th of July, the widest city road in the world. Branching off that road are streets with shops, theatres, cinemas, restaurants and bars in untold numbers. The throb of music and life permeated the atmosphere that balmy February evening and promised all the excitement that young travellers were looking for.

We sampled a small beer or two, in three or possibly four bars, before treating ourselves to a steak in a restaurant. After that, as the sky was getting dark, we tried yet another bar that looked popular. Its doors were open, for the evening was warm, and tango music was wafting out over the heads of the crowd that was spilling on to the street. Everywhere was the sound of good-humoured people enjoying the evening. (In other words, it was indistinguishable from all the other bars in Buenos Aires!)

We ordered Quilmes beer out of a newfound loyalty to the large local brewery. Although the place was crowded, there was some space in the dark interior and we headed for two chairs at the corner of a table where about six young men were already installed.

Our drinks were brought to us in the usual way. Two bottles of beer with glasses atop were delivered, together with a mixture of inexpensive nibbles — mostly pickled gherkin — in two ramekins. Our bill was folded in half and placed under one of these. It was customary for these bills to accumulate throughout the evening and to be settled immediately prior to departure.

We studied the gathered company. All ages and levels of society seemed to be present, judging by the smart city suits and the workman's overalls.

We talked quietly about our success so far. We had negotiated the railways and the underground, eaten a delicious dinner and were now comfortably mellow. Another beer or two would undoubtedly help us decide what to do next.

Before long one of the chaps at the table turned and said, 'Hello.'

This friendly gesture was the welcome opening to a faltering conversation. My Spanish was decidedly limited at that stage and Euan had none at all. Like people the world over, our new acquaintances had a smattering of English, and so we communicated haltingly.

'Yes, it is our first time in Buenos Aires.'

'Yes, we think it is a very beautiful city.'

'No, we aren't tourists; we are here to work but have only just arrived.'

They introduced themselves, Carlos, Raúl, Andrés and so on. We reciprocated, and so the flow of conversation continued.

'Yes, we think there are lots of beautiful girls here.'

'No, we haven't seen any football yet but will soon; there's a good club in Quilmes, we understand.'

'Yes, we know that Argentina will be hosting the Word Cup in 1978.'

I called the *mozo* — the waiter — over and ordered two more beers.

'No, we are most definitely not Yankee gringos! We come from Britain.'

'Ah, okay, I understan' . . . you are Eeenglish, yes? You leeve in Londres, yes?' said Carlos.

'Ach, na! Ah'm n' English! Ah'm frame Oolsta.'

A total lack of comprehension ran round the faces of our new friends.

'Frame Oirelan!' said Euan, surprisingly peevishly, I thought.

Now, given that I struggled to understand Euan, our new friends really didn't have a clue what he was saying, and it seemed to me he had started slurring his words slightly, too, which didn't help. I tried to explain quickly that, in fact, Ulster was a different country from England and the Republic of Ireland. Feeling pleased that I had niftily defused an awkward situation, I was utterly perplexed by the next question.

'Then if you're English, what about Las Malvinas?'

I was a callow youth in those days and didn't have the slightest notion that the Falkland Islands, situated some 275 miles to the east of Argentina's southern extremity, were the subject of disputed sovereignty and the cause of a long-running feud between the UK and Argentina. Even though the Falklands Conflict between Britain and Argentina was not to occur for another decade, I was about to discover the significance of Las Malvinas to the Argentine political consciousness.

I was totally mystified, but Euan knew all about the islands (naturally).

'Tuch! That's complete rubbish, totally stupid!'

Suddenly, the tone of the exchanges with our new friends changed. These lads, who had been all smiles and relaxed amusement during our clumsy conversation, suddenly turned very serious. Body language became tense.

Partly in broken English, but mainly in Spanish, which I translated as best I could, they trotted out accusations against the wicked English pirates who had stolen their islands, rather as the Spanish described Francis Drake when he captured gold they had plundered from someone else.

Euan, who had an unrivalled ability to recite arguments committed to his prodigious memory, vociferously started to demolish their opinions. He pointed out some painful home truths about the acquisition of South American lands by their Spanish forefathers. What had happened to the native populations in the process of acquiring their 'rights' and 'titles' was nothing short of genocide, pure and simple. The British never behaved like that, he said.

I was looking around in astonishment; the situation was quite beyond my experience. Voices were raised and other customers were now regarding us in a less than friendly manner, in marked contrast to the warm welcome I had received in Argentina before that night. I noticed some burly blokes moving in the direction of our altercation and was getting a very uncomfortable feeling that this evening was not turning out at all as I had anticipated.

Euan was getting louder by the minute, emphasizing the validity of each of his points by banging the table with his hand, while completely ignoring my urgent suggestions that we should go. Neither was he taking any notice of the men who were homing in on our table, nor the hostile expressions on the faces around us. It was clear that the lads we had been talking to didn't want to continue with the argument, which had become thoroughly unpleasant. Some were trying to restrain their friends, advising them just to ignore us.

'Okay. That's sufficient! Enough! We don't want to talk with you English any more. Leave it. Enough! Enough!' said Carlos, turning his back on us. But, of course, he had said it in Spanish.

'Okay. *¡Ya suficiente! ¡Basta! No queremos hablar mas contigo. Déjalo. ¡Basta! ¡Basta!*'

Just like when falling off a bicycle, time went painfully slowly, but I was powerless to stop the inevitable crash.

'Wh'ar' you callin' a fockin' bastar', you fockin' bastar'??!!!' Euan screamed at Carlos as he leaped to his feet. In one fluid action, Euan grabbed a beer bottle by the neck and smashed it against the table's edge to produce the most evil, murderous weapon imaginable. Glistening shards of glass flashed in his practised hand as he lunged to grab Carlos with the other.

Instantly, one of the bouncers forcefully struck Euan's arm with a wooden truncheon, causing him to drop the bottle, which shattered on the floor. While two others seized him round his head and shoulders, a fourth had me by the scruff of the neck. All in the twinkling of an eye, chairs and tables were upset, glasses crashed to the floor and, with the assistance of some of the customers, Euan was physically thrown out on to the street. All six foot three of him crumpled to the ground in a heap. I was simply ejected. I looked at Euan in horror. I couldn't believe what had just happened. Slowly and clumsily, he was staggering to his feet. He had an absurd and annoying grin on his face — and then he started to sing! I was forced to the conclusion he was actually enjoying himself.

I was deeply shocked and completely out of my depth. In truth, I was sick with fright. I was a country boy from the gentle Downs of rural Sussex. During the whole of my life I had never had more than a couple of boyish arguments that had ended in a punch-up, and both had been resolved according to Queensberry Rules. I started making my way back towards the station as quickly as I could walk, sobering up rapidly as I gulped in the cooling evening air. By then Euan was standing unsteadily in the middle of the street, shouting, 'Fockin' bastards!' and gesturing with 'V' signs (which are completely meaningless in Argentina) to the front of the bar where the bouncers stood in a row, arms akimbo, forming a human turnstile. I kept moving in as straight a line as I could manage.

He caught up with me before long.

'Hey! Where y'goin'?'

'I'm going back to college!' I answered without looking at him. I didn't want to be with him at all and was debating what I could say to the headmaster if I returned alone. Absurdly, I felt some kind of responsibility for his safety, otherwise I would have lost him in the crowd.

'Why? Don't y' wan' to go on?'

'Go on? GO ON?!' I said in amazement. 'No, I do not! This is not my idea of a good night out!'

'He called me a bastard!' he said indignantly. 'I couldna' ha that, n' could I? Hic.'

'He did not call you a bastard,' I said angrily.

'He said *basta*, which is Spanish for 'enough'. You wildly overreacted.' I was on the point of finishing my sentence with 'you stupid bastard' but thought better of it. I didn't know if there were any more beer bottles lying around.

Sitting in an almost empty railway carriage on the train, Euan dabbed at his face and hands, which had been quite badly scraped when he was thrown out into the road. He rolled up his sleeve to show me the ugly bruise that was developing where he had been hit with the bouncer's truncheon.

'Fockin' bastards!' he muttered. Then, a bit later, he added, 'Ar'ou goin' to stop for a small beer on the way back then?'

'No!' I said. 'Certainly not. I have never, in all my life, been thrown out of anywhere before!'

He looked at me askance, as if to suggest that he had never met anybody who didn't get thrown out of places with regularity.

'Where did you learn to do that with bottles?' I asked, trying to reconcile the two sides of Euan: the erudite intellectual and the drunken psycho.

'Comes with mother's milk where I'm from,' he said in a matter-of-fact tone.

I had to believe it but I was horrified by the thought of the injuries such a weapon could inflict.

He looked out of the window at the passing lights and started singing again.

I did my best to appear not to be with him.

After a short silence, he said: 'You stick wi' me, an' we'll ha' a good time, ma friend!'

46

I could feel my mouth was agape, but the words wouldn't form. What could he mean?

'You've just had some free beers tonight, thanks t'me!' he explained. 'You owe me now, pal!'

It was true, we hadn't settled for the beers. How many? Two — or was it three — each? Worse than that, it appeared I now owed this loose cannon some kind of debt of honour.

I was thunderstruck by the appalling logic. Words failed me completely. I decided it was probably better not to say anything further for fear of making it worse. It was the first time that I felt he had manoeuvred me into checkmate.

Checkmate or not, I determined I would never go anywhere with him ever again. However, I had learned a very valuable lesson. From that time forward I understood both the preoccupation with the Falkland Islands and Argentina's fervent patriotic nationalism.

Now, as I lay in bed waiting for sleep before my early start, a strategy had started to form in my mind as far as Juan Salvador's escape from Uruguay was concerned. It still needed some fine-tuning, but it was beginning to seem possible that I did owe a debt to Euan McCree after all . . .

5

Strange Customs

In which almost everything goes according to plan

My alarm clock rang at five the following morning. Even though I had gone to bed confident I had made the right decision to take Juan Salvador with me to Argentina, I had some apprehensions about what the day might bring. Outside it was still dark, but I got up quickly to see if he had survived the night and grinned broadly when, on entering the bathroom, I saw him so apparently well and pleased to see me. Flapping his wings and running up and down in the bath, he bobbed his head and looked at me, left eye, right eye.

'*Ah, good morning! Sleep well? Have a little lie-in, did we? Better late than never, I suppose. Time to get going now. What are we doing today then? Off on some new adventure?*' he intimated.

'*Today we're going back to Argentina on the hydrofoil,*' I said, '*so best behaviour from you, my friend, and everything will be all right. Just leave all the talking to me, okay?*'

I gathered my possessions, popped Juan Salvador into the string bag and, after a final check of the flat, locked the door for the last time. As I set out for the bus station in the cold and dark, I fervently hoped the Bellamys would never find out that I had cleaned a penguin in their bathroom. I had done my utmost to remove all evidence from the previous extraordinary day and nothing but a lingering smell of sea-bird remained, of that I was certain.

I walked to the end of the road and hesitated. There wasn't another soul around and the only sound was the gentle lapping of the sea, which looked cold and inky-black. The light of a new day was just beginning to brighten the eastern sky. At my feet there were two widely diverging paths and I had to make a choice. After this there could be no turning back. One was straight and smooth, sensible and trouble free. All I had to do was drop the penguin back on to the beach, where he would quickly die of cold as the water evaporated from his saturated feathers and I marched swiftly off to the bus stop. I could rationalize this action by arguing that the penguin would have died regardless and that I had done my best, hadn't I? What more could be expected? But, starting from exactly the same place, there was the other route. It was deeply rutted and mired, it was overgrown with thorns and barbs and so obscured that I couldn't even see round the first bend, but it gave Juan Salvador a chance of life.

Call that a choice? What kind of choice is that?

Two roads diverged in a wood, and I —
I took the one less traveled by,
And that has made all the difference.

49

With resolution in one hand and a disguised string bag in the other, I walked up to the bus stop in the dawn twilight. There weren't many people travelling to Montevideo at that time in the morning and most had a sleepy and unkempt look; I didn't feel out of place with my belongings wrapped in paper and string. When the *colectivo* arrived, not more than ten minutes behind schedule, it was about half full and I took the seat next to a good-looking girl of about my own age, who had smiled at me encouragingly as I embarked.

During my time in South America, bitter experience had taught me that on a half-full bus it is better to occupy a seat next to a companion of one's own choosing, rather than take the last of the unoccupied double seats, allowing Fate to determine one's neighbour. I'd made this mistake once in Bolivia when the next person to board the bus had been a very large (and I don't mean tall) local lady wearing a bowler hat and a colourful shawl. She had three small children and a menagerie comprising numerous hens and a piglet, which were contained, for part of the journey at any rate, in various boxes. Needless to say, out of all the available seats, she took the one next to me. Not only did she occupy much more of my seat than she had any right to, in addition to her own, but I found I was constantly restraining or repelling wriggling, non-house-trained infants and livestock in or out of boxes as she constantly rearranged her responsibilities throughout the remaining five-hour journey.

On this occasion I had all my possessions

comfortably stowed in my rucksack, apart from Juan Salvador in the string bag. I had inverted a large brown paper sack over the string bag and passed the handles through two slits I had cut in its base, so the contents could not be seen. I really didn't want to discuss with anyone why I was carrying a penguin in a string bag. I certainly didn't want the benefit of advice from the legions of doubtless well-intentioned individuals who, given the slightest chance, would line up in long queues to say, 'I really wouldn't do that if I were you!' The die was cast. It was a fait accompli, set in stone. I was going to take that penguin back to Argentina with me, come hell or high water; I simply couldn't leave him behind now to fend for himself, not when he had already demonstrated such reluctance on the beach. Besides, I really didn't think Juan Salvador was long for this world. If the oil didn't get him I was concerned he might starve to death. I knew for certain he hadn't eaten for at least twelve hours and before we met he might not have eaten for days. But if he didn't pull through, it certainly wasn't going to be through lack of effort on my part. That was the end of the matter and I wasn't going to discuss it, justify it, debate it or take advice about it, by, with or from anyone.

The bus journey to Montevideo took less than a couple of hours. It was delightful, travelling through small villages and countryside as both the sun and the temperature rose. Before long, I found myself chatting easily with the pretty girl sitting next to me just to pass the time. Her

51

name was Gabriela and she was going to see her aunt in Montevideo. As we talked about nothing in particular, neither Gabriela nor any of the other passengers were aware of Juan Salvador, standing between my legs in his string bag, out of sight, hidden under the brown paper.

Shortly before arriving at the terminal in Montevideo, a slightly fishy whiff began to permeate the bus. Passengers looked around them, sniffing the air, to see who had unwrapped fish from their shopping. Next, realizing the smell was rather worse than that, they started checking their shoes to see if they had trodden in something nasty and making sure nothing unpleasant had mysteriously fallen into their holdalls. One passenger alone was not engaged in any of these activities — but my cheeks were getting redder. The perplexing miasma held no mystery for me. I was the only person on the bus who knew that the foul odour was caused by penguin guano on the floor but, of course, I decided against enlightening my fellow passengers.

Sitting next to me, Gabriela naturally thought that I personally was to blame for the dreadful smell, and all that implied. She looked at me with a mixture of contempt and disgust, but I couldn't possibly explain. What could I say, 'Don't blame me, it's the penguin!'? It was just too late, the bus was pulling into its parking bay and, besides, I didn't dare trust her with my secret, no matter how pretty she was.

Mercifully, we came to a stop. Without looking to see what had happened or how much guano was slopping around on the floor, I grabbed my possessions and fled, abandoning all thoughts of Gabriela and what might have been.

I disappeared down a side street and followed a sign to a plaza. I came to a pleasant city square with grass, trees and seating; the very picture of a recreational space in a grand, if a little down-at-heel, colonial city. On one side, facing the plaza, was a splendid baroque cathedral, but the best feature of all, for my purpose, was the open air.

Coffee and breakfast were being served on the terraces outside bars and restaurants, and I sat down and ordered the same. I examined the paper-covered string bag and, apart from one small mark, there was no other sign of guano. Manoeuvring the bag to obscure the contents from inquisitive eyes, I lifted the cover slightly and saw, with relief, that Juan Salvador was apparently perfectly happy. He showed no sign of distress and wasn't trying to get away, but stood perfectly still, looking at me.

'*Are we nearly there yet?*' he asked without a hint of an apology for his recent faux pas.

'*What AM I doing with a penguin?!*' I demanded. '*Have you any idea just how excruciatingly embarrassing that was for me, Juan Salvador?*' He continued to look at me, clearly quite unmoved by my ordeal.

I took a deep breath. I had to accept there was nothing to be done about it now. After all, the die was cast, it was a fait accompli, wasn't it? Set in stone! My thoughts came back to mock me. Well, come hell or high water, I'd just have to get

53

on and cope. And besides, I thought, it couldn't possibly get any worse, could it?

'*We're going on the hydrofoil next. That will be fun! But please, no more surprises, all right?*' I pleaded with him.

There was an hour or so before I had to be at the port so I covered Juan Salvador again and settled to enjoy my breakfast while I watched the world go by. My steaming hot coffee arrived and I soon felt its warmth reviving my spirits.

In South America, the majority of boys, while still of school age and when not playing football, were accustomed to supplementing their household income. As a result, the cities were teeming with countless shoeshine boys. This arrangement had the benefit of clean shoes for all, pocket money for the youngsters and an occupation for otherwise idle hands.

One of these boys spotted me, ran over and sat on his homemade wooden box, with its carefully designed handle that doubled as a footrest for clients. By tradition there was rarely any verbal communication in these transactions. The customer accepted the contract by placing his foot on the box. If he considered his shoes weren't in need of attention, he ignored the boy, who silently moved away without offence being taken by either party. I put my foot on the box and he began his work. Vigorously, he cleaned off the dust and, with a parsimony born of want, he applied the smallest possible smidgeon of polish to his brush and set to, polishing and buffing, elbow grease making up for the lack of polish. When satisfied that he had earned his money on the first shoe, the boy would tap the client's foot twice with the back of the brush, which was his signal that he was ready for the other foot.

While he was working on my second shoe, I had started to wonder how I could prevent a deposit of guano on the hydrofoil on which Juan Salvador and I would be travelling for more than three hours. Sitting in that plaza in the winter sunshine, I was smitten with guilt about the mess Juan Salvador had left on the bus. I imagined every policeman in Montevideo would be out looking for the phantom penguin porter and had been issued with a description: 'Fair-haired European wearing a red skiing jacket and blue jeans, carrying a penguin in a string bag.' I did feel ever so slightly conspicuous.

The boy tapped my foot again to indicate that he had finished his task and, after inspecting my shoes, I dropped a few pesos into his hand.

Shoeshine boys didn't hang about as a rule. They would spend a minute or two at most on each customer, whose shoes rarely needed more because of the frequent cleaning they got. They didn't argue about the money either. They'd just flit to the next most likely person they could see. But this boy broke that tradition.

'Señor,' he said.

I looked down in some surprise, much as the beadle might have regarded Oliver Twist.

'Is that a penguin under your bag?' From his perspective he had spotted Juan Salvador's feet. 'Can I see it?'

Satisfied that no one else had noticed us, I lifted the paper bag a little for him to peek

55

underneath. They looked at each other in silence, face to face, for several moments, and as I watched, it appeared as though there was an exchange between these two that transcended words; boy and bird, in a language of their own.

Eventually, the spell broken, almost the same question I'd asked myself only a few minutes before tumbled from the boy's lips: 'Why do you have a penguin with you?'

How much did he know? What had the penguin told him? I tried to answer. 'Because . . . er . . . Well, because . . . ' Each time I started, the words just dried up. Why did I have a penguin in a string bag in the middle of Montevideo? Again I tried. 'Because . . . '

'Because you are English,' the boy prompted me gently, nodding his head in a knowing and even school-masterly sort of way. It was a statement, not a question.

'Look,' I said, wresting the initiative back, 'never mind that. What I need right now is a strong plastic bag that I can put him in. If you can find me one I'll give you fifty pesos.' He looked me straight in the eye. I could see he was weighing up how much money he might make from the increasing number of people who were now on their way to work, against the time it would take him to get a plastic bag and earn the fee. True to tradition, he haggled.

'Make it a hundred?' he said. His cheeky smile was shining through the dirt on his impish face. It was against all the rules of haggling for me to give in too easily.

'Of course — on the condition that you bring

it here, to me, before I finish my coffee,' I said. I'd show him who was boss! Without another word, and pausing only to glance into my cup, he was gone.

I finished my leisurely breakfast and was delighted when I saw him running back across the plaza with a suitable bag. I gave him 200 pesos and he skipped off, beaming from ear to ear.

The *aliscafo* — hydrofoil — that plies between Montevideo and Buenos Aires provides the traveller who has unexpectedly and at short notice found himself with a penguin as a travelling companion with plenty of time to anticipate the possible reaction of the receiving customs officers on the other side of the border. Indeed, because the hydrofoil was extremely noisy, the ride bumpy and the small portholes dirty with exhaust grime, there was little else that passengers could do during their journey but think their own thoughts. Conversation was all but impossible (for which I was thankful on this occasion), as I was reading. Assured of the sensory deprivation of my fellow passengers afforded by the roar of the engines and the blast of cold air during the three hours it took to cross the River Plate, I contemplated the next potential obstacle: I reflected on the Nature of Penguins. Slowly, a stratagem formed in my mind that had begun the night before as I had remembered Euan McCree. I would walk through customs saying 'nothing to declare', while keeping Juan Salvador hidden. Then, if by some miscalculation he were discovered, I would explain that penguins are migratory birds and that I was simply repatriating this *Argentine* penguin, which, due to unfortunate happenstance, had become injured and was only travelling with me while it recuperated. It would then be released back into the wild. After all, that really was my plan, which would be preferable to leaving him at the zoo in Buenos Aires. 'Surely such humane conduct,' I would say, 'can't contravene any regulations?'

By emphasizing the Argentine origin of the bird, I would hopefully appeal to the nationalistic sentiment of any customs officer, which I had learned so recently from the bar brawl was central to local psyche. I hoped I could demonstrate that I wasn't guilty of any charge of bio-terrorism or open to the accusation of the unlicensed importation of exotic species. Thus prepared, I relaxed, ready to allow a beneficent providence to play out its hand; but, I must concede, not without some misgivings.

The Argentine Customs and Immigration Control at that time was not very different from those the world over. Nowadays individuals are given more space and are treated with greater respect. In those days it was not a jolly place.

I was no stranger to the dismal immigration offices down at the docks in Buenos Aires. On my arrival in Argentina I had only been given a visitor's visa. In order to obtain a work permit and permission to reside in the country, it was necessary to get the agreement of the Immigration Department. Naturally, workers from abroad had to demonstrate that their knowledge and skills were superior to those of local labour and of significant benefit to the nation. With all the arrogance of youth, I was of course flabbergasted to discover that the granting of a work permit wasn't simply to be automatic in my case.

Applicants had to present themselves, at the appointed time and with all the necessary documents, to the 'Work Permits' department at Immigration Control at the docks. Those not seen by the end of the day had to present themselves again the following morning and join the queue afresh, day after day after day.

Although living standards in Argentina at that time might have appeared low to people from more developed nations, they were very desirable for the poor among Argentina's neighbours to the north. Accordingly, there were always great numbers of applicants queuing at the docks. However, Argentina didn't want unskilled foreign workers and tried to deter them by making the process of applying for a work permit convoluted, slow and uncomfortable.

There were ways to mitigate the horrors of Immigration Control. Professionals who could show they had been offered jobs by Argentine companies were given preferential treatment. Their employers could send another employee in their stead, with the necessary papers, to make the application for an appointment; however, there was no alternative (other than bribery!) to someone having to join the queue at the docks.

St George's College employed a retired

Englishman who had been born in Argentina to try to smooth the appointment procedure for its employees. For a small sum, Geoff was quite content to pass a few days queuing in the Office for Immigration Control with my passport to arrange my appointment. Success required nothing more than perseverance. The valiant Geoff did most of the queuing for me although, when he couldn't be there, I had to go. Between us we queued for a total of about ten tiresome days, spread over as many months, before I finally had a work permit stamped in my passport.

This time, on reaching the port of Buenos Aires, I entered the vast hall and nervously joined the 'Entrada' line. I showed my passport and visa to the first free immigration officer, who then directed me to the scores of queues waiting to see one of the customs officers. Hundreds of passengers were shuffling along in their lines before placing their belongings for all to see on a table in front of the officials, who questioned them while reviewing their property. All the while, armed troops circulated, observing and supervising the work of the customs officers — all part of the iron fist imposed under the martial law that extended throughout Argentina following the recent military coup.

Although I had a dry throat, I was confident of my practised argument and, by this time, I had shuffling, with Juan Salvador at my feet, down to a fine art. I moved, parent penguin-like, and he simply slid along in front of me. It was all so easy!

When my turn came I placed my rucksack on

the waist-high table in front of the officer that providence had allocated to me. A smart, genial young man in uniform greeted me with a courteous, 'Buenos días,' but before I had the opportunity to reply a second officer approached, tapping his watch. 'Gracias,' said my officer to his replacement, and he departed. How horrifying was this change of fortune? Thank you so much, Fate. The new officer was overweight and had floppy jowls, while his lower jaw was much too big for his head. His dun-coloured uniform was ill-cared for. The top button of his shirt was undone, because he was too big for it to be done up, and his tie was loose. A hand-rolled cigarette, which had gone out, was stuck to his lower lip. His moustache was greying and stained with nicotine, and he hadn't shaved for two or three days by the look of his stubbly grey chin. He wore mirrored dark glasses in heavy frames, so I couldn't see his eyes. No other officer in the place would have filled me with more foreboding.

'Anything to declare?' he demanded.

'No,' I replied to my own reflection in his glasses.

'Where have you been?' he asked with no attempt to sound pleasant or welcoming.

'I have been staying in Uruguay.'

I was obviously just a European traveller and of no interest to him, so he jerked his head sideways, indicating I should move on. I gathered up the rucksack and shuffled. I was through! Oh bliss! Oh joy! Nothing could have been easier. Why had all those doubts been clouding my afternoon? The officer suddenly looked normal, if not angelic, to my eyes.

But I celebrated my victory too soon. To this day I do not know if my elation had communicated itself to Juan Salvador somehow or whether I had simply trodden on his toe. Whatever the reason, at the very same moment I let out a sigh of relief, Juan Salvador uttered the first sound that I had ever heard him make. A loud and piercing squawk of three distinct syllables emanated from the paper bag.

In an instant, the rumble of a hundred conversations subsided into total silence and everybody in the whole building turned to see what had made the extraordinary noise. As the silence grew more menacing, I could feel the increasing warmth of their gaze: hundreds of pairs of eyes settled upon my blushing face. Suddenly everybody was taking an interest in my personal affairs, delighted by the diversion and hoping that their own dark secrets would remain hidden now that the officers were distracted by my discomfort. I imagined all the armed guards loosening their guns behind me and taking out their handcuffs.

'What the devil was that?!' my own officer barked, now alert and scenting blood. He leaned over the counter and looked down at the bag on the floor that I had been trying to conceal.

'What was what?' I said, playing for time.

'In that bag you are trying to hide!'

'Oh, that?' I said. 'It's just a penguin and I'm not trying to hide anything!' I was doing my best to sound both nonchalant and confident, but feeling far from either. The incident on the bus might have been embarrassing, but trouble here was a far more serious matter.

62

'You can't bring animals into Argentina! It is a serious criminal offence to smuggle livestock into this country!'

I had rehearsed my argument and politely set about explaining to the customs guard that penguins weren't 'livestock' at all, but wild, migratory birds and consequently moved up and down the coast of Argentina and Uruguay and even went as far as Brazil without anyone's permission. The reason this particular penguin was using this particular port as a point of return to the Argentine was due only to an unfortunate injury it had sustained, which required that it travel in company with me temporarily. On its recovery, I explained, it would be free to continue migrating at will.

I went on, too scared to stop talking for fear of what might happen next. Under normal circumstances the penguin would not dream of troubling the republic's customs officers. Besides, I couldn't possibly be guilty of smuggling because it was an Argentine penguin and so I was doing nothing other than repatriating the bird. (I was very pleased with that line and was sure it would play particularly well. It didn't, of course.)

The officer listened to my argument poker-faced, obviously failing to understand the impeccable rigour of my logic. His sour expression didn't change. I had a chilling thought, too, that the military government that had recently seized power might not grasp the finer points of *habeas corpus* for penguins and, at that precise moment, I didn't feel too confident about its application to people either.

'Come with me,' he said, crossing to a private room and beckoning ominously with his podgy forefinger. Picking up the rucksack and Juan Salvador's bag, I followed him with a sense of impending doom. He closed the door heavily behind me. There was a bad smell in the little interview room and no outside sound penetrated its solid walls.

'Show me,' he said. I placed Juan Salvador on the table and removed the paper bag. Juan Salvador looked at me and then at him.

'Oh! It really is a penguin!' he said in astonishment. He seemed surprised.

'I told you it was a penguin. They are migratory birds and do not usually go through customs as a rule, I imagine. This Argentine penguin is staying with me only while it recovers from an accident.'

There was an uncomfortable silence while he thought for a moment or two, eyeing both Juan Salvador and me.

'Are you sure it's an Argentine penguin?' he asked dubiously, stooping to look directly at Juan Salvador. 'That makes a difference, of course.'

'Oh, yes!' I said emphatically, 'There isn't the slightest doubt about that. He was hatched near Río Gallegos.' This is in the extreme south of mainland Argentina. 'Look at his markings. You see, I'm an expert on penguins,' I said, bluffing with the supreme confidence born of knowing Juan Salvador wasn't about to denounce this outrageous falsehood.

The customs officer looked at the penguin for several more seconds, stroking his chin.

'Mmmm,' he said. Juan Salvador returned his look, not with the curious cocking of his head from side to side, but antagonistically face to face. The officer blinked first. Finally, he appeared to reach a conclusion.

'Yes . . . I see now . . . of course,' he said.

After a quick check to make sure the door was firmly closed, he leaned across the table so that his face came close to mine.

'You have dollars?' he hissed quietly between his teeth as he grinned hideously and looked furtively over his shoulder, all the while rubbing his thumb against his index finger in a gesture familiar the world over.

That was when the penny dropped. Of course, I hadn't contravened any laws or regulations and he didn't care about the bird at all. He simply wanted a bribe and thought I could be frightened out of a few bucks. Although I did have a few greenbacks, I wasn't going to pay him for the privilege of looking after a penguin that had caused me so much trouble. Besides, he had just weakened his case considerably and to my advantage. Checkmate! It was my turn to win for a change. I took a pace or two backwards as though in disgust.

'How dare you ask for a bribe?' I said, with all the pomposity a twenty-three-year-old could muster. 'I shall complain to the authorities! Where is your commanding officer?' I knew that the threat of complaint to the military so soon after the coup would get a reaction. I turned and started for the door.

'Keep the bird and look after it yourself!' I

said, looking over my shoulder. 'He likes sprats. Lots of them. Oh, yes, and I wouldn't put your fingers anywhere near his beak if I were you!'

But before I had reached the door there was a guttural, threatening command.

'Stop! Don't take another step, señor!'

Had he pulled his gun? Had I made a terrible mistake and pushed my luck too far this time? I froze immediately and slowly started to turn round. He had moved well away from the penguin on the table and his hands were now clasped behind his back.

'Take the bird! You can't leave it here!' he said, before adding with an ingratiating smile, 'There's no need for you to tell anyone about this, is there? Is there?'

So I collected Juan Salvador and disappeared into the crowd before the officer could change his mind or mention the guano that had been left on the interview-room table.

The next leg of my journey — from the port to the underground, to the rail terminal at Constitución station and then on to Quilmes on the FCNGR railway line — took us less than an hour and passed without incident. Then we had a mere fifteen-minute bus ride and we were home.

With a cheerful '¡Hola!' I greeted the guards on the college gates, trying to sound as normal as possible, and after promising to tell them about my adventures once I had taken a bath, I hurried on towards my flat, hoping I wouldn't bump into anyone on the way.

Oh! How great was the sigh of relief I heaved when I kicked my front door shut behind me and put Juan Salvador into the bath. He looked well, considering he had been in a string bag all day.

'Well, here we are, home!' I said as he took in his new surroundings. But he wouldn't look at me. 'What's the matter with you?' I asked.

'Río Gallegos indeed! I'll have you know I was hatched on the Falkland Islands!' was the unmistakeable reply.

'That's quite enough from you!' I said. 'You have caused far more trouble than you're worth for one day. ¡Basta! And besides, why did you squawk at the Customs Office? You embarrass the life out of me on the bus and then you nearly get me arrested!'

He finally turned to me with a butter-wouldn't-melt expression and I smiled because, in spite of it all, the hell and the high water, I had brought him home to Argentina.

'Río Gallegos indeed!'

6

You Shall Have a Fishy

*In which I get far more than I bargained
for on a shopping trip*

I rubbed Juan Salvador's chest and his
prominent breast bone seemed razor sharp. I
wondered when he'd last eaten. The markets
would still be open if I didn't dawdle so I took a
few thousand pesos in notes from my hiding
place and set out for Quilmes. I grabbed my
bicycle, pumped up the tyres (which had to be
done before every journey) and, in no time at all,
I was on my way.

For the past six months, since my arrival, I had
been forced to learn very quickly how to survive
an economy in dramatic inflation.

On my arrival at Ezeiza International Airport
in Buenos Aires, I had been met by my new
employer, the headmaster of St George's, and
taken to the college in one of the city's ubiqui-
tous Ford Falcons. On the way I was plied with
information about the history, geography and
economy of Argentina and, among other things,
I learned I would be given an advance on my
salary. After we had eaten, the bursar showed me

69

to his office and I was given one and a half million pesos in crisp new notes (printed in London by De La Rue, I noted). I was told to go into town that afternoon and buy all the essentials I could possibly need.

Quilmes had been a comfortable suburb of Buenos Aires when the college was built, but fashions change and the northern districts had become more desirable. Now it had the distinct feel of an urban hinterland. The roads were made of thick concrete, which had cracked into great slabs resembling ice floes. Electricity cables were knitted between poles in an apparent free-for-all, while manhole covers jutted high above the pavement at odd angles. Like all Argentine towns, Quilmes was built in city blocks of one-hundred-metre squares, with the edges of the corner buildings bevelled at forty-five degrees, often with a door, to avoid sharp angles on street corners.

Some buildings were obviously shops, but others were more ambiguous. They appeared to be shut up securely with rolling metal curtains, which protected the doors and windows and were an integral part of their construction. It made them extremely secure but not very attractive. Every block had a repair workshop or breakers' yard for something or other, with stacks of domestic appliances, motorbikes and other assorted bits of metal and rubber or bric-a-brac that cascaded on to the pavement from the dark interior. Grimy, boiler-suited workers were always busy smoking and chatting.

How would I go about spending a 100,000-peso note? What was it worth? I had brought all the immediate everyday essentials in my hand luggage, and everything else was coming by sea. I wasn't aware of anything that I needed and was at a loss to know how to spend the money.

It came as quite a surprise to discover I knew nothing practical. Not only did I not know the price of anything, I had no way of estimating the price of anything. How much do you expect to pay for a beer if you have fifteen notes totalling 1.5 million pesos in your pocket? Although I knew the exchange rate, it didn't really help. Manufactured items were much more expensive than at home, while labour was cheap. Teachers could easily afford to employ a maid, a cook and a gardener in their homes, but buying a car was usually out of the question.

And so I spent my first afternoon exploring the suburb of Quilmes. I had lunch. That was easy: there was a menu and price list outside the restaurant and after that I had a pocketful of small change. I bought some beer, fruit, coffee and milk, and went back to college for tea.

Later that evening, I saw the bursar again.

'Spend all your money?' he asked.

I hadn't, I admitted, because I didn't know what I wanted. He became really quite fierce. I had committed a cardinal sin, it appeared.

He told me it didn't matter what I wanted: I had to buy whatever I could get hold of and then publish a list of what I had and barter with it back at the school. He said I might only get half the value on the second day because inflation was running at about one hundred per cent a month.

Why hadn't he explained properly in the first place, I wondered? Not for the first time did it occur to me that communications are not a strong suit of bursars.

The following day I went out first thing and spent. Relatively few of the shops were open. Those that were had prices that were changing continuously. In general, shops were closed unless the owner needed some cash or knew he could replace his stock.

In the mini markets, assistants went round changing the prices not by three or five per cent a day, but simply doubling the marked prices every couple of weeks. If a particular price was too high it would be self-adjusting as inflation would catch up over the next few days. Assistants even changed the prices of items placed in shopping baskets, sometimes right at the till, when the cashier would look at the marked price and say, 'It costs twice that today!' One could take it, leave it or try to haggle, which was sometimes successful.

I bought jeans that wouldn't fit and shirts I'd never wear. I bought coffee sets and toothpaste. I bought absurd quantities of cheap cutlery sets with varnished bamboo handles in hideous green plastic zip-up folders. (Arguably any quantity of cutlery with varnished bamboo handles in hideous green plastic zip-up folders would be absurd and I bought a dozen place settings!) I bought hardware and rolls of cloth and films for cameras I didn't have. I bought enough mosquito spirals to last a lifetime.

I did manage to spend almost all the money,

however, and had no trouble in bartering my goods later on, even the ghastly cutlery which (I was intrigued to find) was acquired by the bursar!

Before long I discovered that as a foreigner I could buy US dollar travellers' cheques, which meant I didn't have to go on these absurd shopping expeditions every month. Another consequence of inflation was that, by law, wages and salaries had to be paid to employees in the middle of the month. This was an attempt to protect workers. Why, the argument went, in times of high inflation, should the employer have the advantage of payment in arrears?

Even better, holiday pay had to be distributed on the last working day before a holiday. That meant we were paid for the whole of the summer break at the beginning of December — summer being December to February in Argentina. Now, to receive three months' pay in advance is pretty good but, when I collected my pay from the office that December, I found I had four months' money. When I queried this, I was told it included my *aguinaldo*. 'Ah! Of course!' I said, not wishing to appear more stupid than necessary, and went to ask the other ex-pat staff what an *aguinaldo* was. They told me that it was a Christmas bonus.

Eva — 'Evita' Perón — Juan Perón's second wife, who wielded immense political influence during his first administration in the 1940s, had been instrumental in introducing many financial reforms such as these which were intended to benefit the workers. No wonder she had been

73

worshipped by her *descamisados* ('shirtless ones'), as she referred to the labourers in electrifying speeches and broadcasts that galvanized the support of the 'downtrodden' poor for the Perónist cause. Unfortunately, the financial catastrophe of that administration ultimately did far more harm to those same workers than they understood at the time.

During my stay in Argentina I was fascinated by inflation. Some people got used to living with it and had found ways of using it to their advantage while the Perónist government kept interest rates low. House owners would proudly explain to me that they had bought their homes on a mortgage and that, after only a few years, their repayments were now down to the equivalent of the cost of a couple of pints of beer and would be half that next month, and so on. I knew that by contrast there must have been people losing out somewhere, because inflation was supposedly an economic illness, but it would be some time before I understood more clearly how it worked.

Once at the market, I was relieved to see that the fishmonger had no shortage of sprats and I queued impatiently, Juan Salvador's rumbling tummy on my conscience. The old woman in front of me, dressed from head to toe in black and with the countenance and temper of a bulldog with toothache, was struggling with the price of the catch-of-the-day and while I was

74

sympathetic to her cause, I had penguins on my mind.

Because inflation had been raging, the decision had recently been taken to 'revalue' the Argentine peso. Uruguay had done something similar and a 'new' Uruguayan peso was now valued at 1,000 old pesos. Since everything cost multiples of thousands or tens of thousands or hundreds of thousands, division by 1,000 was simple — one just left off the 'thousand'. Thus a beer costing 10,000 'old' pesos cost 10 'new' pesos after the change. Everyone understood and the transition was easy.

Anxious not to be seen to be imitating its tiny northern neighbour, however, Argentina instead chose chaos by rejecting common sense. One new peso was worth just 100 old pesos. This elderly woman standing between me and Juan Salvador's sprats was the latest casualty to what was swiftly becoming general pandemonium. Dividing prices by 100 caused problems for many people. The beer that had cost 10,000 'old' Argentine pesos now cost 100 'new' pesos, which was not so simple to calculate in one's head, especially after one has had a few of them after an evening out. Worse, someone had the bright idea to overprint existing bank notes with new denominations and it was done in such a way that neither the new number nor the old was legible.

The fishmonger was doing his valiant best to reassure the woman that the new prices were correct and that she wasn't being swindled out of her life savings. The situation wasn't helped by the fact that he was getting confused himself, and arguing with other queuing customers about how best to convince the old lady. It was going to take all night, obviously, and I wanted desperately to get back and feed Juan Salvador. Oh, hell! I was on the point of screaming with frustration, but retained sufficient self-control to restrict myself to muttering discreetly, or so I thought, under my breath and in English: 'Oh! For God's sake, dear, get your arse in gear.'

Instantly, this elderly lady stopped speaking and rounded on me, eyes ablaze, and rapped me repeatedly on the chest with her black purse as her shawl slipped off. She continued to hit me even as I attempted to pick it up for her. Then, in the most superior and refined of tones, she said: 'Young man! How dare you speak to me like that!'

Oh, the embarrassment! It was as though my grandmother had overheard me use a rude word when I was ten, and I hadn't intended to be unkind to her.

Of course, it wasn't until later that I worked out what I should have said, which was, 'Madam, please excuse my unpardonable solecism.' And then, with a debonair flourish, I should have insisted on paying for her fish myself to make up for the distress I had caused. However, in my embarrassment such savoir faire completely eluded me on that occasion, but I have it saved and ready for the next time she is dithering in front of me in the queue.

On my return, Juan Salvador welcomed me back by running up and down in the bath. He was a very inquisitive bird and stretched up tall to see what I was carrying.

'*What's in the shopping bag then? Let's see!*'

I placed the bag of sprats in the handbasin and, sitting on the side of the bath, I took one by the tail and waved it in front of him. He took no notice, so I bumped his beak with it and tried to dangle it across his nostrils.

'*Come on!*' I said. '*Don't you want some of these delicious fish, fresh from the Quilmes market? These sprats are the best money can buy! Show some gratitude, bird!*'

He closed his eyes and shook his head rapidly with a shiver of disgust as he pressed his beak down into his chest in a gesture of revulsion.

'*No! Take it away, nasty limp thing. I only eat fish!*' he was saying as clearly as if he had spoken in words. There was no mistaking the fact that he was not interested in these sprats. So what to do next? If he didn't eat quite soon the end would not be long in coming. Could I force feed him?

I took his head in my hand and pushed a finger and thumb into the corners of his beak so that it opened. As soon as I could, I placed the fish into his mouth, held him still to taste the sprat, and then let go. A violent shake of the penguin's head sent the sprat flying across the bathroom, missing me by inches. It hit the wall behind my head and slithered down to the floor. He wiped his beak against his chest, but otherwise didn't move. He certainly didn't appear to be frightened of me or

77

what I had just done. With unruffled dignity, he carefully set about preening himself.

Not to be thwarted, I tried once more. Holding his head still, I pushed a fish deeper into his mouth. Following another violent shake, a second fish joined the first. He looked at me closely.

'Didn't they have any fish in the market then?'

'They are fish, Juan Salvador.'

'No. Fish wriggle and live in water and swim, but I can swim faster! Don't you even know that?'

I hadn't gone through all the acute embarrassment, inconveniences and drama of the past day to be defeated now, so I tried a third time. Holding his head erect and beak open, I pushed a third fish into his mouth, but this time I pushed it really far down the back of his throat. In fact, I shoved it deep down into his gullet with my finger. Then I let his head go and watched. His little eyes, usually protruding, were now closed and he had stopped breathing. Had I stuffed the fish down his windpipe in error? Would he choke to death on a sprat? Could one perform the Heimlich manoeuvre on a penguin? Was it possible to retrieve a fish that had gone so far? I massaged his gullet to encourage him to swallow. His eyes had become curiously concave under their lids, as though a vacuum had developed inside his head. I felt alarmed. He stood perfectly still, eyes shut tight. Seconds passed. Then he began to wobble, and I was on the point of trying to pull the fish out, when he swallowed. I saw the bolus move down his throat, his eyes open and return to normal.

I breathed deeply and wiped away the cold sweat that had formed on my brow. Throughout all this, he hadn't struggled, tried to get away or objected in any way that I could identify. He stood still now, watching me, left eye first, then the right; comprehension slowly dawned in them. He was no longer wiping his beak against his chest with his eyes downcast; they sparkled and looked directly at me, left eye, right eye. He looked up at the basin, then back to me, and indicated as clearly as if he had the gift of speech:

'Ah! Sprats! In the blue and white plastic bag! So why were you waving them under my nose? Do you think things smell under water? Really! Are there any more? By Jove, I'm hungry! Come on, chop, chop! I haven't eaten for days, or have you forgotten?'

Taking another fish by the tail, I held it above his head and, before you could say 'Juan Salvador', he had snatched it from my fingers and swallowed it whole. I yanked my fingers clear in response to his lunge and the heavy clack of his closing beak. There was no second chance for anything that came within range of those jaws.

Once started, Juan Salvador wanted to make up for lost time. He swallowed fish after fish as fast as I could pick them up. It seemed he had to close his eyes in order to swallow. I tried offering a fish by the tail first to see what he would do but this was no challenge. In a single movement he took it, flipped it, caught it head first and down it went, following the others. In the space of the next ten minutes the entire bagful of fish disappeared down his throat and his tummy bulged noticeably. He even ate the two fish from the floor. Between sprats, I rubbed my fingers against his plumage to clean them and to promote, I hoped, the restoration of waterproof feathers.

I shut the bathroom door that night and went to bed feeling more hopeful than at any stage since I had found him on the beach the previous day. In the morning, I was pleased to note that he appeared to be well and was standing away from the guano that was conveniently deposited at the plug end of the bath.

'*You need to do something about cleaning your bath, you know!*' his imperious look suggested.

After breakfast I pumped up my tyres, hopped on the bike and returned to the market. I was pleased to find that the fishmonger still had plenty of sprats although he was astonished that I wanted another kilo quite so soon.

'It's for the penguin,' I said.

'Oh, of course! Silly of me not to guess. So you'll be back tomorrow for some more then?' he said with a wide grin, which died rapidly as I replied: 'Certainly! I expect to be buying sprats every day from now on.'

Juan Salvador only managed a couple of dozen for breakfast, but had a few more every time I came and went, so by the end of the day he had polished off a second kilo of fish, and any doubts I had about the state of his insides were allayed. I had a very efficient guano maker installed in my bath.

7

Upstairs Downstairs

*In which Juan Salvador takes up residence
and hosts a house-warming party*

Preparing for the return of the students gave
me plenty to do at the college, while eating in the
bachelors' dining room four times a day lent
structure to daily life. It was at dinner on my first
evening back that I asked the few colleagues who
had returned from their holidays about the
habits of penguins, on the pretext of having seen
some on my travels. I hoped the real reason for
my curiosity wasn't apparent. At that stage I
wasn't prepared to reveal that I had taken a
lodger into my flat.

Despite some enthusiastic responses, I learned
nothing useful that I hadn't already discovered,
with Juan Salvador's help. The library revealed
no new information either when I searched the
shelves for books on local fauna. It did appear,
however, that a diet of fish alone was sufficient
for a penguin, which was most reassuring.

The boys were accommodated in three large
three-storey buildings located in the southern corner of the college campus, about seventy to each.
The thirteen- to sixteen-year-olds had dormitories and common rooms, while the seniors had
study-bedrooms. Each boarding house was run

by its housemaster with two assistants. Because I was single I occupied one of the staff flats that formed an integral part of the building and the housemaster's house was built on to one end.

My flat in School House was on the second floor (or the third if you're American, North or South). Either way, it was on the top floor and I had to climb two flights of stairs to reach it. A door adjacent to the flat allowed access to an open-air roof terrace above the housemaster's residence. It measured about thirty feet square and had a parapet of eighteen inches high around the edge (approximately, as it turned out, the height of a Magellan penguin). The floor of the terrace was tiled and had a slight incline, for drainage. It was equipped with a table and chairs and a hose to clean it but otherwise it was quite bare. The only access to the terrace was via this door and, when it was shut, there was no alternative exit for a penguin or a person.

On the day following our return to college I put Juan Salvador out on the terrace while I had a bath before breakfast. It was with considerable consternation that I noticed the enamel on the bottom of the bath where the guano had been was no longer a smooth vitreous surface but rough and actually quite abrasive in patches. I was astonished by the damage and careful never to slide up and down in the bath again for fear of injury! I also resolved not to touch guano with my fingers or get it on my skin. If it could corrode bath enamel like that I didn't like to think what effect it might have on human tissue.

What luck Juan Salvador hadn't damaged the Bellamys' bath!

The time had come. I had to tell the college staff about Juan Salvador. It was quite apparent that he wasn't about to drop dead; in fact, on the contrary, he appeared to be thriving on a diet of Quilmes fish market sprats and he seemed to be utterly content living at my effort and expense. He didn't appear to be looking for ways to escape or to be pining for the company of other penguins, which allayed my concerns for his welfare. His friendly, enthusiastic and inquisitive behaviour was really very endearing. He hadn't made a sound since the episode with the customs officer, but I didn't altogether trust him not to, so before he was discovered I had to seize the initiative. I didn't want it to appear that I was hiding the penguin or that I had a guilty conscience about keeping him in the college.

Following breakfast, I went to the Sewing Room in search of the one person whom I thought would be my greatest potential ally.

'Maria, I need your assistance,' I said, after exchanging the usual pleasantries at the beginning of a new term.

'*Por supuesto, señor*, how can I help you?'

'Maria, I have found an injured penguin and I was wondering if you could — ' I began.

'You have found a penguin?! Here, in the college?'

'Could you spare a moment?'

Maria was the college housekeeper, in charge of all the cleaning and laundry. She had worked at St George's since she was thirteen years old and was by then a shade over seventy. The laundry was done by hand, by women of all ages who lived in the neighbourhood and came in daily. Maria's responsibilities had increased over the years until eventually she had become the most senior, whereupon she was rewarded with the job of housekeeper. She managed all the female cleaners and laundry staff. There were no pension arrangements for people like Maria, so she had to keep on working until either she dropped dead or she became too feeble; at which point she'd have to rely on somebody's charity. She would never be able to retire because her savings never accumulated any value.

It was in getting to know people like Maria that I became better educated as to the losers in an inflationary economy. The poor, the *descamisados*, were rewarded with money that rapidly devalued, leaving them nothing to show for it. The 'rich' were the beneficiaries because their assets maintained or increased in value as a result of labour they paid for with worthless money. Inflation was clearly transferring enormous wealth from the poor masses to the rich few. It was Maria and the thousands of 'shirtless ones' like her who effectively paid the real cost of the smart suburban houses in Buenos Aires.

My intriguing disclosure had aroused Maria's curiosity. She immediately put down the task she had in hand and followed me as I set out towards my rooms.

Maria was only an inch or so over five feet tall, had an enormous bosom, suffered terribly from arthritis and bunions, and was as bow-legged as it was possible to be; while she might not have been able to catch a pig in a passage, fortunately there was very little demand for that particular skill at St George's College.

As we walked at Maria's pace I began to tell her about my adventures during the holidays. She had long been troubled by her knees so she compensated by walking with a rolling gait (not unlike that of a penguin). Slowly, she climbed the stairs, hauling herself up using the banisters, puffing with each step, and her smile of achievement as she reached the summit was as warming as sunshine. For her, the joy of the things she could do outweighed the woes of those she couldn't. In all the time I knew her I don't believe I ever heard her grumble about her own lot and I loved Maria like a grandmother.

Nothing was ever too much trouble for 'Santa Maria' as she became known, for she had the kindest heart of anyone I have ever met. She loved the boys and wanted to mother them, to their gratitude, amusement and annoyance in more or less equal measure. And she wanted to mother the young teaching staff, too. Once, during a strike in the laundry, the boys had to do their own washing but it was all I could do to prevent Maria doing mine herself. The laundry ladies won an increase in pay after two or three weeks, principally because some of the boys' mothers were so horrified at the thought of their darling sixteen-year-olds washing their own underpants (or possibly not washing them) that they wrote in protest and everything returned to normal in a wonderfully pragmatic Argentine way.

When I opened the terrace door, Juan Salvador immediately looked at us and, just as I had anticipated, it took him two seconds or possibly less to melt Maria's heart. She eased herself down the two steps and he ran over to her and looked up into her face. She was so concerned when I told her about the oil and tar that, naturally, she wanted to mother Juan Salvador, too. Of course, Juan Salvador, as we were soon to discover, could take all the mothering that was on offer! She sat on the parapet and ran her gentle fingers over the contours of his shoulders.

I suggested that she might like to give him breakfast and within moments Maria was attending to Juan Salvador's morning repast. After each fish he shook his head, flapped his wings energetically and vigorously wagged his tail in appreciation. This master fisherman had hooked a new convert and she became besotted by him. Thereafter Maria would frequently take tasty morsels out to him and together they would put the world to rights.

My little round of disclosures continued when I went to find the headmaster to report the temporary stay of a penguin on my terrace. I reassured him that on my next free day, provided he had recovered sufficiently, I would be taking him to the zoo in Buenos Aires, and I said the same to Richard, the housemaster. As a result, Juan Salvador and I received a nearly continuous dribble of visitors throughout the day.

At dinner in the mess that evening I recounted the story of my skirmish with a penguin in Punta del Este and explained why the bird was now living on my terrace. My colleagues listened to the narrative of his rescue and cleaning with glee but when I revealed his name, George interrupted: 'No, no, you must call him Juan Salvado — 'John Saved'.' The others agreed unanimously that it was a more appropriate name than Juan Salvador (John Saviour); and so it was that his name became Juan Salvado among his intimate friends, although he remained Juan Salvador on formal occasions.

Naturally, the teachers wanted to see him too, and so, after dinner, my companions accompanied me to the terrace and were introduced. My peers sat on chairs and the parapet and, as the port passed to the next person on the left, the bag of sprats passed to the next on the right. Juan Salvado captivated the assembly by running to each person in turn as they held up a fish for his delectation. As his tummy filled, so his eating slowed, but he was evidently enjoying having company. Only when he became less active did my colleagues' attention begin to wander and the conversation of the humans moved on to include other topics of common and pressing interest (such as the alleged antics of the army's machine-gun-wielding boy conscripts or the chances of Quilmes FC in the Cup).

That was the first of so many times that I observed how completely at ease Juan Salvado was in the fellowship of humans. He wasn't intimidated by their height or inhibited in any discernible way. He would greet visitors to his terrace with warmth and, as far as I could tell, a genuine desire for friendship. No, that doesn't do it justice at all — he was ecstatic when people came to call. A guest would feel as though he had just arrived at the house of an old and valued friend after a long and arduous journey. Juan Salvado had all the charm of a precocious young child but, unlike that of precocious young children, the charm of Juan Salvado wasn't ephemeral; in fact, it never waned. Possibly his behaviour was more like that of the perfect host at a grand society banquet, His Excellency Don Juan Salvador de Pingüino. Witty, urbane and dressed immaculately in white tie and tails, with a confidence born of a noble ancestry, superior learning and wider experience, His Excellency circulated among his guests. As he approached, other conversations were broken off to attend to him. Then he would make each one of his visitors in turn feel that it was the pleasure of their company alone he was seeking, if only he were not compelled by the unyielding laws of etiquette to move on and talk with his other invitees. And so it was that, although literally the humans fed him with fish, figuratively Juan Salvado had them all eating out of his hands.

On that first night the penguin had been standing by me looking around the assembly and appeared to be wondering if, possibly, there was room enough for just one more sprat, when I noticed his eyes flicker and his head nod. Shortly after, I saw he was fast asleep, although still standing up, gently leaning against me, replete and apparently totally at peace with the world.

The following day was the last before the return of the students so while time still allowed, and now he was no longer living as a fugitive, I decided to see how my new compadre would cope with a walk on the fields and some exercise more motivating than the confines of the roof terrace allowed.

The grounds of the college were quite extensive. There were many large open playing fields, which were lined with great eucalyptus trees. There were also quiet places of denser vegetation, more like the shady corner of a domestic garden. I carried Juan Salvado out on to the grass, where we walked slowly under the eucalyptus trees. Wherever I went, Juan Salvado followed, staying within a few feet of me at all times, just as he had on the beach in Uruguay. With growing confidence I walked faster and the penguin ran at full speed to keep up. For penguins, running involves holding their wings out and rotating their bodies to maximize the distance of each pace; few people can resist laughing at the sight. I walked unhurriedly most of the time, carefully observing his behaviour. Although Juan Salvado examined the grass, leaves and twigs on the ground, he never strayed far from me. We met several college employees on our tour and I explained the presence of my new companion. While no one made any overt criticism, I thought I detected some mild implication that I had behaved eccentrically in some way, but I expect I was just being over-sensitive. Juan Salvado was the living proof that my intervention on the beach in Uruguay had been the best course of action available to me.

Our first walk around the grounds must have

been a mile or more and I was watching carefully for signs of fatigue or other indications that begged '*Carry me!*' but none came. At the time I was surprised but, on reflection, it occurred to me that penguins have the stamina to migrate thousands of miles each year and propel themselves far greater distances than humans do, so a gentle walk round a rugby pitch probably wouldn't be much of a challenge.

In those days Calle Guido — Guido Street, the metalled road from Quilmes — ended at the gates of the college. At this point it turned into a rough dirt track, which continued for another mile and a half down to the river. The land on both sides of the track belonged to the college; to the north, the flat open ground was marked out with rugby pitches and was surrounded by beautiful jacaranda trees.

There are many species of jacaranda growing throughout Central and South America and all those I have seen are lovely. Some are small and grow no bigger than bushes, while others become large trees. Those that had been planted around the rugby pitches were perhaps forty feet high. They had been carefully tended to form a large spreading habit that gave a maximum amount of dappled shade, quite as wide as the height of the tree, where both spectators and players could shelter from the sun. In springtime the jacarandas wore massed tresses of breathtakingly vivid bluebell-coloured, trumpet-shaped flowers, which engulfed the entire canopy of the tree — their vibrant, striking blue even eclipsed the sky on a perfect, cloudless day. In their season, the flowers quite overwhelmed the pale green filigree foliage that contrasted so strikingly with the very dark, hard and deeply fissured tree bark. The delicate leaves remained attractive throughout the summer, long after the flowers had faded. Towards autumn the fruit developed, forming small golden-yellow, grape-like bunches that positively glowed in the light of the setting sun and clung on long after the leaves had fallen. To my mind, jacarandas are among the most beautiful of trees and the penguin's progress beneath them made an unforgettable picture.

The fifty or so acres of land to the south of the dirt track contained all the college buildings, as well as many more games fields. Today the relentless march of suburbia has surrounded the school. However, in those days one could walk between the high chain-link fences that surrounded the two pieces of land making up the college campus, on which spiky shrubbery was encouraged to grow, and follow the track that ran through the neglected scrub, past a few scattered dwellings, all the way down to the River Plate; a good half-hour's hike, but very much longer if accompanied by a penguin.

The dwellings between the college and the river couldn't quite be described as smallholdings but they were more sophisticated than those of a shanty town and had been constructed from building blocks and timber which the inhabitants had 'salvaged' from around the district. Their dwellings were not attached to the usual utilities so they had to live and bring up their families without electricity, running water or drainage.

They would grow a few crops on little patches of land, keep hens and pigs, and eke out a living by doing such jobs as could be found in town. The college employed some of these locals as cooks, cleaners, laundry women and maintenance workers.

I often enjoyed an evening walk down to the river and, after I had acquired an interest in penguins, I enquired of the people who lived there whether they had ever seen birds like Juan Salvado on that part of the river. 'Never,' was the answer. The sprats, and therefore the penguins which feed on them, would keep well out to sea to avoid the vast fresh water discharge from the river. Thus the penguins must swim some 200 miles in the open sea between departing the Argentine coast and arriving in Uruguay. The more I discovered about penguins, the more remarkable and engaging I found them to be.

The Río de la Plata is enormous, as wide as the English Channel. Imagine standing at Dover looking south; the temperature is 30° Celsius, the water is warm, muddy and brackish, the vegetation subtropical and the sun is going backwards through the sky. (In the southern hemisphere the sun travels anti-clockwise.) Now you have an idea of what it was like to stand at the end of that dirt track on the bank of the River Plate.

Although not a salubrious area, the boys of the college were perfectly free to take a stroll down to the river or walk into town alone. Looking back from a time where civil liberties have been restricted in ways unimaginable then, it seems like a golden age of personal freedom, even though the political situation was close to anarchy. Some of the students in the college came from the richest and most influential families on the continent and yet they could mix relatively freely with the residents of this area, or the *bajo* as it was known, who were among the poorest. The vulnerability of the boys was discussed at staff meetings but, apart from the armed guards on the gates and simple tennis-court fencing around the perimeter, happily no additional security measures were necessary.

When we arrived back at School House after Juan Salvado's introductory tour of the college, I walked up the two steps to the front door. The penguin, however, bumped into the first step as though he hadn't seen the obstacle. He bounced back and sat down. I picked him up and carried him inside. He was always perfectly happy to be carried and never struggled to get away. Once through the front door, I put him down again.

My flat was at the top of a grand flight of solid wooden stairs. I began my climb, paused and turned to see what he would do next. Again he bounced off the bottom step, but this time he studied the obstacle, first with one eye, then with the other, until suddenly he appeared to understand. Without further ado, he walked back to the step and hopped up and forward, landing on his belly on the first tread. In doing so, he bumped his head on the next riser. Undeterred, he stood up and hopped on to the next step. This time he landed diagonally across the step on his tummy and so measured his full length without banging his head. Immediately he repeated the process, landing on the other diagonal, and thus he followed me, zigzagging up the next few steps. I ascended a bit further and he followed.

Hugely impressed by Juan Salvado's astuteness, I naturally wanted to see how he would manage descending, so I ran back down the stairs. Without hesitation he launched on to his belly and tobogganed, bump, bump, bump, down the flight of stairs at great speed, landing on the polished marble floor at the bottom in that prone position. He came to a sliding stop and stood up. While he was never destined to be the fastest ascender of stairs, Juan Salvado could come down a single flight faster than anybody, effortlessly negotiating the two right-angle turns in the construction of the staircase. Later, I was to discover that, unbeknown to me, the boys had arranged races against the bird and he won every time! When I heard about these contests, my blood ran cold and I banned them peremptorily, appalled by the possibility that some boy might accidentally land on the penguin as he attempted to jump down half a dozen steps in a single leap, not only crushing the bird to death, but breaking his own neck as the eviscerated carcass slid from under his feet and he tumbled to the foot of the stairs. I shuddered with fear at the very thought of it. But as I prepared for the beginning of that term I had no presage of the levels to which boyish skylarking with the seabird might escalate.

'His Excellency Don Juan Salvador de Pingüino.'

8

New Friends

*In which the students return to find
an unexpected guest*

It seems to me that there is a very particular
polish that is only ever used in schools, and its
odour permeated the atmosphere as the babble
of students shattered the quietude of the
dormant boarding houses. The tramp of feet and
crash of trunks bulging with uniform and sports
gear as they were dumped unceremoniously at
the ends of beds by their owners heralded the
true beginning of a new seventeen-week term.
The college was juddering back to life. I was not
sorry to see the return of the boys that spring. It
was becoming clear that Juan Salvado loved
company and with over three hundred people on
campus, it was certain he would not be short of
friends.

The college was home not only to the students
in term time but also to many of the teaching
staff and their families together with the nurses
of the sanatorium, and in that close-knit community everybody knew everybody by name. Each
of the classes at St George's had fifteen or so
students and dormitories were of a similar size;
the dining hall could hold the entire school comple-
ment and did so three or four times a day; and

Jorge, the chef, knew how to feed the Argentine appetite of that young army. The chapel, too, was large enough to include everybody and we met there, with only slightly less frequency and enthusiasm, for servings from the chaplain.

I stood at the top of the stairs and directed the traffic, wondering how long it would be before any of the boys looked out of the glazed terrace door. I didn't have to wait for long. An intelligent lad, with a mop of jet-black hair and an irrepressible smile, wandered that way and looked out over the fields towards the river, feeling, no doubt, the mixed emotions common to everybody at the start of a new term. He was from Peru but his grandfather had been a Russian émigré.

It was several seconds before something close at hand attracted his attention.

'There's a penguin out there!' he said quietly. He looked away and then back, almost pressing his nose against the glass. Turning his head, he saw me and repeated, 'There's a penguin out there!'

'Oh, I expect it has just flown in for a rest as it migrates south for the winter,' I said. Cognitive contradiction was a teaching style I liked — saying untrue things that forced students to challenge the ideas they were presented with.

Igor frowned and looked back towards the terrace, but spun round instantly, the word 'No!' dying on his lips as he saw my expression. He grinned, too, in acknowledgement of the joke. 'May I go out there?'

'If you are very calm and gentle, yes.'

Gingerly, he opened the door and stepped down on to the terrace. I moved to watch. Juan

Salvado flapped his wings in greeting as Igor walked slowly over to him and stooped to stroke his head. The penguin ducked and moved away but soon he was egging the boy on, playing to his audience. Igor looked at me. 'Can I tell the others?' he asked.

Like wildfire, news that there was a penguin on the terrace ran around School House and a crowd of boys eager to know the truth about this rumour jostled excitedly at the terrace door. Initially, I regulated the numbers allowed outside at any given time, fearing that Juan Salvado might be overawed by the attention, but we soon learned there was no apparent upper limit to the number of admirers that particular penguin deemed to be enough.

The boys were delighted to be allowed to feed him and very soon I had volunteers, especially from the younger ones, to feed Juan Salvado, to wash down the terrace on a regular basis and to buy fish from the market each day. Responsibility can so often bring out the best in youngsters and there was no shortage of willing helpers ready to let the 'best' be brought out of them by tending to the needs of Juan Salvado.

Only seeing penguins in their natural environment can give one a real understanding of the meaning of 'gregarious' as an adjective. Humans, in general, can be described as gregarious, but penguins crowd together in untold numbers with no apparent concept of personal space. Having said that, perhaps an English boarding school (or one in South America), mirrors life in a penguin rookery more than most other forms of human society.

Rising early in the morning, streams of students would leave their boarding houses to go to the dining hall for breakfast. They'd return to collect the essentials for the morning lessons, then the tide of boys would ebb out again to attend Chapel and their classes. A mid-morning break would see them flood back to the house to substitute books and apparatus appropriate for the next set of lessons. At lunchtime they'd come back to the house to drop their belongings in their lockers before rushing out again on their way to the dining hall. Hunger for victuals satisfied, they'd head back to their dormitories for a siesta. Refreshed, the tide would flow out again to partake in games and physical exercises of many and various sorts. Back at their respective houses, they'd shower and collect their books, hungry once more for the pearls of wisdom that would fall from the lips of my colleagues during the day's final set of lessons. Then in they'd come again to leave their books before going to the dining room for their last meal of the day. Finally, they'd return to studies and common rooms for prep, after which every boarding house would buzz with boys enjoying their only free time of the day before a final shower and bed. Such is the routine of boarding schools.

So, there was a regular coming and going of youngsters, which might have been designed for the amusement and delight of a penguin in residence. On every occasion that he heard boys going by, Juan Salvado would animatedly run up and down his terrace, straining to see, and invariably some of the boys would go out on to the terrace and talk to him or feed him fish.

While the free time of boys in a boarding school is very limited, it was quite possible for an enthusiastic chap to make twenty minutes available between the end of games and the start of afternoon lessons and there was never a shortage of boys volunteering to go to the market and purchase sprats. After the first few days, Juan Salvado had settled down to a regular daily diet of only half a kilo of fish, so it was perfectly possible to maintain a goodly stock in my fridge with only three trips a week to the fishmonger. The reward for getting provisions from the market was the privilege of feeding Juan Salvado and washing the terrace.

Usually a small group of up to half a dozen boys would sit on the parapet of the roof terrace and feed their new friend. At the beginning of a meal Juan Salvado would snatch and swallow fish as fast as the feeder could pick sprats from the bag, and with scant respect for the fingers of the unwary or inexperienced. (I should say here that nobody suffered permanent injury from Juan Salvado's eagerness for fish.) However, towards the end of a meal he would slow down as swallowing became more of an effort. Observant benefactors would notice when Juan Salvado was full and stop feeding him, but occasionally, schoolboys whose fingers were no longer in jeopardy of amputation and who were lost in conversations of their own would continue to feed him until he couldn't swallow at all and a fish tail was sticking out of his beak.

Thus replete and totally contented, Juan Salvado would stand in the centre of the little group of boys and gaze lovingly up at them, drinking in every word. Then, overcome by an over-tight waistcoat and the warmth of the late afternoon sun, he would nod off, falling sound asleep while leaning against the helpfully vertical legs of the boys. And there he would remain until they left. The more considerate among them would gently lower him on to his fat belly where, child-like, he would sleep on without stirring. The less thoughtful just got up and ran off when they suddenly noticed they were late for their next appointment, leaving Juan Salvado to topple over. On such occasions he would simply shake his head like an indulgent grandparent and then settle down again to continue his afternoon nap. Such was the life of Juan Salvador the Penguin, snoozing on peacefully while the rest of us returned to our labours.

9

Treasure Trove

In which I sacrifice something precious

One afternoon, shortly after Juan Salvado had taken up residence on my terrace, I was in my rooms when my attention was suddenly caught by the sound of excited chatter. I assumed that it emanated from a group of boys walking towards the house, but it had a frisson that was unusual in some way that I couldn't quite identify. I was preoccupied with the radio and the lengths of wire attached to the aerial that I had draped around the room in an unsuccessful attempt to tune in to the BBC World Service for news from home. It was usually a waste of effort at that time of day but occasionally my endeavours were rewarded with the homely tones of British newsreaders, sibilantly modulated by the ionosphere.

The group reached the house and walked up the steps. I heard the front door open and close and the voices slowly grow louder as the party climbed the stairs and eventually came to a halt outside my flat. The radio had failed to deliver and curiosity got the better of me so I went to investigate, anticipating the knock. Opening the door, I found a boy with a triumphant expression on his face and the object of his elation, a large, old and grubby galvanized iron basin, in his hands. It was oval in shape, about three feet long by two feet wide and some nine inches deep with handles at either end.

'Cortés,' I said, full of admiration, 'you are quite brilliant! Where did you steal it from, not some poor old lady's garden?'

'I don't steal nothing!' he said indignantly.

'No, I was only joking,' I said, 'but you're still brilliant. Where did you get it?'

The beaming smile returned to his face. 'I was walking back from town and saw it among the junk in one of the workshops. I asked how much they wanted for it and was told that if I could get it out I could have it.'

'Didn't the gate guards stop you?' I asked. They had clear instructions to prevent the boys from bringing rubbish into the college.

'They wanted to but when I said you needed it for the penguin and had sent me to get it, they let me through. You did send me to get it for you, didn't you?'

'Ah! Yes!' I said. 'Now I recall! Well remembered! You'll go far, Bernado Cortés!'

In the few weeks that Juan Salvado had been at the college, he had adapted to life on the terrace as a duck to water. The table provided him with shelter, if he needed it, from the sun or hail, and he loved the daily shower that he was given either by me or the boys. A gentle stream of water was arranged by letting the end of the hose dangle from the table and Juan Salvado could stand under this homemade waterfall.

The ritual was always the same. He would dip his beak into the flow for a second or two and then shake his head energetically. After repeating this two or three times, he would begin to wash his face and neck with one foot while balancing on the other. Then he would move on to clean other parts of his body. It was astonishing how much he could groom with his feet; he seemed to have pliant rubber bones that allowed for any contortion. Next he would move away from the running water and attend to his feathers with his beak, starting at his neck and working at every bit of himself, until he reached his tail, which he wagged spasmodically, rapidly and vigorously throughout the process. At this signal we would towel dry him gently, which would set him about preening his feathers anew.

We had wondered about how much water penguins usually drank or if their water requirement came wholly from the fish they ate. Consequently, Juan Salvado had never been left without water in a large saucepan. College water was extremely saline, so I wasn't worried that he might be deprived of essential salts, even though I never actually saw him drink. I was reassured that it was available to him should he need it.

Bernado Cortés had been inspired when he spotted the large galvanized basin in some grimy corner of a workshop in Quilmes. It would allow Juan Salvado to have a bath and to be fully immersed in water, if that was what he wanted; to cool himself when necessary as the heat of the summer increased. It helped to ease my mind about Juan Salvado's immediate well-being. His feathers showed no sign of regaining their impermeability.

As Cortés held out his prize for me to inspect, it was immediately obvious that the basin had been well used. I could imagine it for sale in a hardware shop or general store at the end of the nineteenth century, hanging from a hook on a ceiling beam, bright and new, with a hand-written price tag made of buff manila card and attached with hemp string. It had been bought, I didn't doubt, by some pioneering family of the time, along with other barest essentials. I pictured a thin young man dressed in baggy dungarees, with his wife of just a few days, purchasing only the indispensable items that their pockets could afford and which wouldn't overload their horse-drawn, and almost obsolete, cart. Some sheets of corrugated iron, wood, nails and a hammer, fencing wire, a pick, a shovel, matches, flour, seedcorn, potatoes, a white enamelled jug, some ammunition and this tin bath. These few things, together with their love and determination, would be enough to start a homestead of their own from scratch, but only just.

There, Juan Salvado's bath had been at the heart of their domestic life as they struggled to tame the land, make a living and create a new farm south of Buenos Aires. Perhaps it had served in the kitchen for preparing food and as a sink for washing up after meals. Doubtless, it had done service in the laundry and in the bedrooms, too. New babies would have been bathed in it and water heated in it. Covered, it would have made a dry, pest-proof store. As the household grew, prospered and climbed the social ladder, it was slowly relegated to ever-more menial jobs,

105

such as a feeding trough for the pigs and bucket for slops. Eventually, after a lifetime of duty, battered, scraped and beginning to rust, it went as part of a job-lot in a farm auction when the family home was sold. And so it had passed through different hands, until finally it languished, unwanted, in a breaker's workshop in Quilmes. But Fate had one more noble calling for it and arranged matters so that a passing schoolboy spotted its potential that particular afternoon.

'It's exactly what we need!' I congratulated him. 'Well done! Put it out on the terrace and give it a wash.'

Willing hands bore the trophy out on to the terrace for cleaning. Mud, grime and spiders' webs were swept away under the full force of the water from the tap and Juan Salvado stood beside the basin in order to supervise. Satisfied with the progress, he rubbed his head against his chest in the fine mist that bounced from his feathers, and again I marvelled at his astonishingly flexible neck which allowed him to turn his head upside down in the process. The rainbow created by the sunbeams in the spray around the penguin made for an unforgettable image.

In no time at all the loose material had been cleaned off and the basin, filled with bright, clean water, stood ready to do service once more.

There were some blocks of *quebracho* wood close to hand. They had been brought from the abundant stocks in the woodsheds to hold the hosepipe down on the table and to stop it from snaking off when the tap was turned on. The word *quebracho* can be translated as 'breaker of hatchets'. As its name suggests, it is an exceptionally hard, dense wood which sinks in water and is of no great practical use except as a fuel because it burns like coal. Its density made it useful as a counterweight, and now, placed against the outside of the basin, the blocks made a stairway for Juan Salvado to climb up and into his bath, while a similar arrangement placed inside the basin gave him a means to get out again. Being *quebracho*, they didn't float but stayed where they were put, on the bottom, under the water.

When all was ready we stood back to see what the penguin would make of this new addition to his terrace furniture and were ready to congratulate each other on a job well done as he rushed into the water with delight and swam around; but Juan Salvado did no such thing. He took no interest at all in his new tub, he simply continued preening. He didn't even look at the tin bath, which was most unusual. Generally, any new object on his terrace would immediately elicit his curiosity.

The watching boys were decidedly crestfallen.

'*¿Porqué no usarlo?*' asked one.

'*¿No le gusta?*' responded a second.

'Speak in English!' I reminded them. When the boys were not in Spanish classes the college rules were quite inflexible on this matter.

'*Sí*, it not like him!' stated a third.

'Give him time,' I said. 'It's just unfamiliar to him.' I tried to be encouraging but, like the boys, I was very disappointed by the penguin's reaction.

Suddenly one of the boys said, 'I know! I know what he want. He want *yelo*!' And turning to

107

me, he asked, 'You have *yelo*?' in the perfectly normal Spanglish that infiltrates the Anglo-Argentine vernacular.

'What do you mean 'yellow'?' I asked, 'Yellow what? Yellow paint? Of course he doesn't want paint, stupid boy! Why on earth would he want yellow paint?' The boys loved my imitation of the ex-colonial Colonel.

'No, not paint, just *yelo* by its own! So he feel at home!' he said, grinning.

The other boys laughed and translated for him: 'Just say 'ice'!' they teased.

'*Si*, ice! *Hielo! ¿Tiene?*' — 'You have?'

'Ice! Where? In there? It wouldn't make a jot of difference to put a few ice cubes in that amount of water! Not the slightest!'

'Yes!' 'Yes!' '*Si!*' they chorused. Suddenly all the boys thought it was a really good idea and the key to the problem. 'Please! You have?'

'Well . . . ' I hesitated. 'I do have a little ice in my fridge, but only a tiny amount, not much. It won't make any difference at all. He's not an Antarctic penguin so he won't be the slightest bit influenced by a few ice cubes.'

Besides, it was very nearly six thirty and time for the bell that summoned the boys to go to the dining room for dinner. It heralded one of the few peaceful moments in the college day when I sometimes enjoyed a quiet gin and tonic on the terrace with colleagues, and my precious ice made from bottled water was an imperative part of the ritual. I hoped I had poured cold water on their idea.

'Oh, please!' they begged in such a pitiful way

that I felt I had to make the supreme sacrifice. Reluctantly, I went into the flat, took out the small tray of ice from the freezer compartment and slyly slipped a couple of cubes into a glass, which I put back in the fridge for later.

'There you are,' I said, handing over the plastic ice mould. 'But it won't make any difference, none at all. You'll see.'

Just at that moment, the dining-room bell rang out across the campus.

'Right, there we are, off you go! Stop messing about here! Just leave him alone and I expect he'll discover the bath for himself,' I said. 'You can come back later.'

'*Momentito, momentito!*' they implored and threw the handful of ice into the water, where it was going to melt in a few seconds and make no discernible difference to the temperature of the bath at all.

But, at that instant, Juan Salvado stopped his preening, looked up and, just as though the ice was precisely what he had been waiting for, hopped up the steps like a veteran who had done it a hundred times before, stepped into the water and began to wash.

The peals of laughter that greeted this action were infectious and I told the boys to get along to eat at once. Off they ran, laughing all the way. Voices mimicking, 'It won't make a jot of difference!' drifted up to the terrace and were met with fresh gales of laughter every time it was repeated until they reached the dining room, a hundred yards away.

I poured myself the promised G&T and joined

Juan Salvado on the terrace for a sundowner. Sitting comfortably in the warmth of the setting sun, I raised my eyes and my glass to the penguin.

'*Good health, Juan Salvado!*' I said, '*Salud!*' and sipped. And as I toyed with the ice in my glass, it chinked against the sides. He returned the salutation with '*Bottoms up!*' by bending over and shaking his tail as he pecked at an ice cube. He submerged his wings in the water and splashed furiously.

'Juan Salvado did no such thing. He took no interest at all in his new tub, he simply continued preening.'

10

Terrace Talk

In which a problem shared is a problem halved

The college water supply was practically undrinkable because of its salinity and the pipes furred up so rapidly that they had to be replaced every few years. We had been told that the works in School House would interrupt our supply and that the maintenance men would need access to our accommodation, so it came as no surprise to me when, one siesta time, three men arrived at my flat in order to measure the pipeline. They finished the job in less than ten minutes, thanks to the simplicity of my kitchen and bathroom, but next they asked if they could tackle the terrace.

One might have expected the mission to be accomplished in only a minute or two by the trio, one with a pencil and paper, one with a tape measure and the third acting as foreman — there was only one short length of pipe out there, after all — but Juan Salvado had other ideas.

My flat had a window fitted with blinds that overlooked the terrace and, whenever Juan Salvado had visitors of his own, I couldn't help but overhear the conversations that took place without anyone being aware. Now I watched as Juan Salvado insisted on checking the measurements for himself and before long the three men were sitting on the parapet explaining to the bird the precise specifications of the job they had to do and how much more satisfactory he would find the water pressure once they'd worked their magic. I had been given a fraction of the same information!

I had become accustomed to this kind of anthropomorphism. I myself was guiltier than anyone when it came to attributing human characteristics to the penguin. I was relieved and amused to find that other people reacted in much the same way as I did, and I had to stifle more than a few laughs as the simple measurement took over half an hour with Juan Salvado's help.

A day or so later I was a bit surprised when I answered a knock at my door to find a number of the groundsmen on the threshold to my apartment, their collective gaze aimed directly over my shoulder. All became clear when they explained they wanted to see Juan Salvado, not me. They were delighted when I asked if they'd like to give him his lunch and the men trooped out on to the terrace to feed him some sprats. In no time at all they were discussing his walks around the college, assuring him that a new lawnmower was on its way to improve the quality of the grass. They hoped he would approve.

The cleaning ladies of the house didn't require my fish or my permission to visit Juan Salvado. I had made it clear to all of them that they should visit him as frequently as they pleased, but no doubt they would have done so anyway — this had been their domain long before it was mine. Just as with his other guests, conversation moved

113

swiftly past opening pleasantries and complimentary remarks and on to the issues of the day. Inflation and the inadequacy of their pay was possibly the subject most frequently aired by the laundry ladies, closely followed by gossip about the other members of staff.

Maria became a frequent visitor too, tottering out on to the terrace every time her duties took her past the door (and after the arrival of Juan Salvado, she made sure her duties took her there almost daily). Sitting on the parapet, resting her weary legs, she would unburden herself from all the goings-on among the domestic staff or she would raise other problems that vexed her, such as shirts scorched during ironing or the inevitable dalliances between her 'girls' and the boys. '¡Ay ay! Juan Salvado,' she would lament. '¡Madre de Dios! What are we going to do?'

I overheard many such conversations between visitors and bird, both in English and Spanish (interestingly, he was quite fluent in both languages), as people went out to pass the time of day. Of course, the reason he enchanted everybody, adults and youngsters alike, was that, as with any good pastor or patrician, Juan Salvado was such a good listener, patiently absorbing everything that was said to him, from observations about the weather to secrets of the heart, and he never once interrupted. He looked people straight in the eye and always paid such close attention to what was said that his guests were inclined to talk to him on equal terms — they thought him a wise old bird. He even looked the part; with his 'dog collar' and long black cape he resembled nothing so much as an elderly, diminutive, genial Victorian country parson, who was rather troubled by gout. In fact, with a cross round his neck, he could have been a bishop.

This impression of giving his undivided consideration to whatever was said came from the way Juan Salvado cocked his head, alternately focussing with one eye and ear at a time. His visitors could trust his discretion absolutely and they could rely on his unconditional support. Inability to speak was no obstacle for Juan Salvado; his eyes gave him all the lucid eloquence of a great orator. Possibly, I mused, it was the fact that his diet was fish, said to be so good for the brain, that gave his intimates confidence in the thoughtful wisdom of his answers.

'¡Ay ay! ¡Madre de Dios! What are we going to do, Juan Salvado?' began Maria's conversation one day as I was sitting in my rooms, marking students' work. 'I don't know, Juan Salvado, these girls are so stupid! But then, so are the parents! Fancy letting that boy bring valuable cufflinks back to college. Anyone could have stolen them! Or the stupid boy himself has simply forgotten where he put them and that's most likely! Those cufflinks are worth three months' pay for my girls. I suppose one of them might have thought she could get away with stealing them. Now we'll have the police in! That's never happened before, Juan Salvado!'

I peered through the blinds. It transpired that one of the boys hadn't removed the gold cufflinks from his shirt and when he discovered his mistake he had gone to the laundry to ask for their return. Nobody had seen them. These cufflinks were valuable not just because they were gold, but because they were a treasured family heirloom. The upshot was that the boy had accused the laundry ladies of theft and the boy's parents were insisting that the police be called in.

Fortunately, most incidents within Maria's jurisdiction were less serious and more predictable and, in the end, all the issues were resolved, of course. Damaged shirts were invisibly mended (Maria's skills with a needle were renowned) and even the cufflinks were discovered thanks to Santa Maria's efforts and restored to their rightful owner. And so it was that Maria ran her domain. She brooked no interference. As a tigress protects her cubs, so she ruled with a rod of iron but a heart of gold. The boys could do no wrong, and neither could her girls. If her girls did transgress, then she would sort it out and woe betide anyone else who thought to interfere. She discharged her responsibilities in the way she saw fit and she gained admiration and respect for her decisive determination. And through it all, Juan Salvado listened carefully and was a tower of strength.

But it was the boys themselves who were Juan Salvado's most frequent visitors. They usually arrived in groups to discuss the unfairness of some imposition or the tactics for the next rugby game. Occasionally, though, a boy would wander out on to the terrace alone. One conversation in particular sticks in my mind, from the day when Julio Molina, in pensive mood, came to consult the oracle.

116

'¡Hola! ¿Qué tal? Hello, Juan Salvado, how are you today? What beautiful weather we have been enjoying of late! What a magnificent view you have from here. Oh! You can see all the way to the river.' Following the preliminary pleasantries, the tone became more conspiratorial. 'Actually, I'm glad to find you alone, Juan Salvado, because I could do with your advice right now and I — well, I don't know who else I can ask. You see, I've met this girl . . . Where? Oh, at my cousin's house. And I, er, well, um, I think she's really pretty and, well, I find myself thinking about her all the time and I've been wondering if I should ask her out . . . er . . . but . . . well, um — eh? What!? Sorry? Oh! *Magnífico!* . . . You think that I should invite her out? Ah! Oh! . . . Wow! Really? You do? Oh, that's wonderful! Oh, *muchísimas gracias*, Juan Salvado, *muchísimas gracias!* I will! I'll go and do it right now.'

And off he went happily on his way, glad to have had his previous intentions endorsed by such a reliable and trusted friend.

11

A Visit to the Zoo

In which a difficult decision is made

Ever since Juan Salvado had failed to swim off and look after himself on that first day in Punta del Este, it had been my intention to present him to the zoo in Buenos Aires. There, I reasoned, he would benefit from the company of other penguins and from the expert attention of the keepers. After some weeks living with the bird, I had become greatly attached to my new friend, as had so many of my colleagues, but I knew I needed to explore further options. The three months of the summer holidays offered an unparalleled opportunity for me to travel extensively and I wanted to make the most of them. However, I had taken on the responsibility of looking after a penguin and I had to make suitable provisions for his well-being before I could go off on any more adventures.

It had certainly not been my intention to keep a penguin as a pet or indeed to have any kind of pet while I was in South America. I was young, adventurous and living abroad. I wanted to do as much exploring of that vast, wild and romantic continent as I possibly could. The college afforded me a base from which I could operate, an income, notwithstanding the inflation rate, and more than four months' holiday every year. Living in college, everything I needed was provided: four meals a day in the refectory and a superb four-roomed flat with all my cleaning and laundry thrown in. That meant it was possible to save almost every peso of my salary. With the money I saved, I purchased a motorbike, an ideal form of transport for penniless explorers like me who had a wish to emulate Che Guevara's mode of travel, if not his politics. However, motorbikes are definitely not compatible with explorers who have penguins as travelling companions.

It had become my custom to use the bike to visit various landmarks on my days off. In a boarding school, residential members of staff have duties to perform throughout the term and, to compensate for having to work on Saturdays and Sundays, we had a day off during the week. It was on one of these days, in early spring, that I finally had the opportunity to head into Buenos Aires and visit the zoo.

Following the recent *coup d'état* that had ousted the administration of Isabel Perón and brought General Jorge Videla's military government to power, everything started to work properly. Trains ran on time and the economy of Argentina stabilized. Holding foreign currency was no longer a criminal offence but inflation remained high and, consequently, come payday, everybody made a beeline for their banks to exchange pesos for hard currency — which really meant buying US dollars.

The bike was *hors de combat* yet again — it was proving to be highly unreliable — and so on this occasion I had taken the train from Quilmes into the city and completed my own currency transaction at the bank before I finally set off for the penguin enclosure at the zoo.

The usual attractions of a zoo held no interest for me at all and, on arrival, I passed the lions and the elephants, the alligators and the hippos with hardly a second glance as some very uncomfortable questions about keeping wild animals in such confinement exercised my mind. I made straight for the penguin pool. I was looking forward to seeing penguins displaying their black and white coats properly, because Juan Salvado's tummy feathers would not get their true colour back until he moulted.

I was in for a shock. Seven unhappy-looking birds flopped around a shallow pool, which didn't look deep enough to reach the tops of the keepers' wellington boots, while the entire enclosure was no bigger than Juan Salvado's terrace. There was some shade, and they had all found room within it, but they were not behaving like the penguins I had seen living free near the ocean. They were lying around listlessly, at some distance from each other and with their heads drooping disconsolately.

It was a very warm day in the city, and in the wild these birds would naturally spend their summer months in the far south of Argentina, where it is much cooler. I felt disappointed.

I had seen great rookeries of penguins in the wild, on the coasts of Patagonia and Chile. The individual birds behaved like Juan Salvado, constantly alert, curious and interested, except when asleep, and even then they always looked content. These birds in the zoo did not appear content; indeed, they looked thoroughly miserable.

It was just at that moment that a keeper came by, and I asked if I could quiz him about penguins. He was a cheerful type, happy to oblige.

Yes, penguins were perfectly happy on a diet of fish alone and didn't need anything to supplement their diet.

Yes, penguins needed to swim for exercise and to maintain health but it didn't have to be seawater.

The bigger the pool, the more satisfactory it would be. The zoo couldn't keep a greater number of penguins because they didn't have enough space.

Yes, Buenos Aires was a bit too hot for penguins to live in all year round.

Yes, he was on his way to feed the penguins now.

Yes, they were fed several times a day. They would eat, on average, about two hundred grams of fish a day.

I was greatly reassured by the keeper's confirmation that the regime for looking after Juan Salvado at the college was apparently satisfactory, but if he were to stay much longer I needed somewhere for him to swim. The pool at the zoo was hardly big enough for the penguins to swim properly, but I wanted Juan Salvado to have as natural an experience as possible.

The keeper took his leave, unlocked the gate to the enclosure and went into the small building disguised as part of the rocky landscape. He reappeared a few minutes later with a bucket of what looked like chopped-up mackerel. In a dispirited and disinterested sort of way, the penguins watched him as he approached.

I, too, watched with anticipation. Lethargically, the penguins took the fish he offered before slumping down again. Their behaviour was so very different from Juan Salvado's that I was shocked. He would rush up and down as soon as he heard anyone approaching, and would greet them with a vigorous bobbing head, which brought his eyes to focus in turn on the face of his visitor and also on what they were carrying for him in their hands. When offering fish, Juan Salvado's patron was always very careful to hold the sprats by the tail to keep his fingers well away from the penguin's powerful, unerring and razor-sharp beak.

It was clear to me by now that the behaviour of these penguins wasn't what I had seen in the wild. Possibly the heat in the enclosure in Buenos Aires Zoo didn't suit them — and it wasn't yet the height of summer. By comparison, Juan Salvado was living on a terrace at St George's at the southern edge of the city. The comparatively rural location and the breeze that blew constantly from the river kept the temperature there a good deal cooler than at the zoo. In fact, Juan Salvado seemed to enjoy the sunshine at the college and could often be seen, when no visitors were present, standing stock-still facing the setting sun as though extracting the last of the warmth before bedtime.

So there it was. I had gathered the information I had come to collect, seen the conditions in the zoo and now needed time to consider my options.

I left the zoo, made my way back to the centre of town and, on a whim, went to Harrods, the overseas branch of the London store, to have a cup of tea. I needed to think about the best course of action for Juan Salvado and, of course, to look at things I couldn't possibly afford.

The waitress brought my tea and I declined the cucumber sandwiches that she had pressed me to take. Rather than admit I couldn't afford them, I insisted I really wasn't hungry. I started eating the sugar lumps as soon as she left.

I poured some tea from the pot into my cup and, stirring my unsweetened tea for the sake of the illusion, I began to consider the ramifications of my visit to the zoo. Juan Salvado gave all the appearance of being considerably more content with his lot at St George's than the birds I had just seen. He ate much more than his counterparts and had many more 'friends'. He was always alert, active and so pleased to see company. I had checked my facts with the keeper and had the evidence of my own eyes. Reluctantly, I was coming to the conclusion that handing him over to the Buenos Aires Zoo wasn't what I wanted for him, unless no other options presented themselves.

If I were to keep Juan Salvado at home, at St George's, rather than send him to the boarding school for penguins in Buenos Aires, was I really acting in his best interests? It was all very well to decide against the zoo, but it was clear from the keeper's advice that I would have to find somewhere for Juan Salvado to swim. A solution to that problem wasn't immediately obvious. What would I do if he were to become seriously distressed as the heat of the summer drew on? What was the alternative? I had to consider the possibility of releasing him back into the wild, but that would not be so easy. Could I take him back to Punta del Este in Uruguay? Back through customs? Really? What other options were there? The nearest sea I could take him to, in Argentina, would involve a six-hour train journey to Mar del Plata, some two hundred and fifty miles to the south. I had done most of the journey once before, by mistake; I had fallen asleep after a particularly good night out in Buenos Aires. I awoke at an unfamiliar station in the small hours and, luckily, was able to catch the early train back to Quilmes.

I would be able to take Juan Salvado on a train and get him to the sea if I took food and an early-evening departure so the journey wouldn't be too warm; it was feasible, but would there be any penguins when we got there? If there were, would they accept him into their colony? Would there be any sprats for him to eat? What if he again refused to leave me? That line of reasoning didn't seem very promising.

The nearest rookeries of wild penguins that I knew of were at Península Valdés and that was getting on for a thousand miles away by road. The practical difficulties of getting him there would be formidable. The best option would involve taking both the motorbike and the penguin to Bahía Blanca by train, and then riding the bike to Valdés. I could only hazard a guess as to the journey time, while I continued to stir my tea. The first leg, to Bahía Blanca, might take fourteen hours, and then the second leg, by bike, another ten. I couldn't see the round trip taking less than four whole days and that was without allowing for contingencies, which prudence would counsel against. Then, supposing I did get him there? What if I couldn't find the colonies? Even if I did, would it make any sense to abandon him there with no guarantee he would be accepted by the incumbents?

No, the only reasonable thing to do, I concluded, was a reconnaissance of Valdés as soon as I could and to make no irreversible plans until then.

That impulsive refreshment in Harrods tea room meant that I had to take the last possible train back to Quilmes to get me there in time for my late-afternoon duty in the college. This, in turn, set me on a collision course with a *force majeure* and illustrated the necessity of preparing for all eventualities in Argentina at that time. Juan Salvado would be the least of my problems in the heat of what was to come.

After an exile of eighteen years, Juan Perón began his third term as president of Argentina in 1973 at the age of seventy-eight. His third wife, Isabel Perón, became vice-president. The infighting between the various Perónist factions and the terrorism mounted by the Montoneros (an urban guerrilla movement) caused great turmoil.

Bombs killed and maimed indiscriminately while 'drive-by' shootings, intended to be more targeted, still produced 'collateral damage'. I wasn't prepared for the chaos of Argentina in the days after I first arrived, despite being warned of the 'culture shock' by my new employer. Every morning the newspapers printed long lists of people who had died on the previous day in different outrages.

When, in 1974, Juan Perón quite suddenly died, Isabel became president. She was hopelessly out of her depth, badly advised and had none of the political shrewdness or guile that had propelled her predecessor, Eva, to the top. Argentina slid towards total anarchy. Although the people I knew represented a wide range of Argentine society, there appeared to be a fairly general consensus that things had become so bad that only the army could restore order.

I vividly recall a particular television programme shown during the time Isabel was president. A TV set had been left on in one of the common rooms and, as I was passing, I went in to turn it off. It was only by chance that I saw the transmission. I watched in utter disbelief. It featured a birthday party, one that appeared to be a child's celebration, with jelly, hats and musical chairs. People laughed when food fell on the floor, blew noisy party whistles and sang 'Cumpleaños Feliz' when the candles were blown out. But the 'birthday girl' was none other than the President of the Republic of Argentina, Isabel Perón, and the revellers displaying infantile behaviour were members of the government. They were all in denial. These frivolous party antics were being televised nationwide against a background of daily bombings and heinous murder.

Living in an atmosphere engendered by terrorism ensured that the majority of people worried only about themselves. The result was that nothing was reliable. Shops might or might not open; trains might or might not run; electricity supplies weren't dependable. Not unreasonably, self-preservation was everyone's first priority. One of the most noticeable results of this was that people did not turn up for work or did not work to the standard that would normally be expected. Employment had become a relatively low priority. The government of Isabel Perón failed to maintain law and order or to fulfil the basic duties and functions of a government, yet it appeared that the army was reluctant to stage a coup and impose order.

It was a military coup, in 1955, that had ended the earlier Perón administration and, although the army had soon handed power back to a civilian government, the shadowy hand of the armed forces was never far from the helm in the 1950s and 1960s. This caused much public resentment and explains why the military held back for so long in the 1970s. They were waiting for near-universal public demand for the army to 'save' the nation.

Throughout 1975, calls for intervention grew as the situation deteriorated. These intensified month by month and, by 1976, it was widely expected that the military was 'just about' to seize power, and yet, day by day, no move came. By March of that year, rumours of a revolution were rife. On the 21st I wrote a letter to my parents:

A short note to get it off quickly. Rumours are flying around and no one seems to know anything for certain, but according to the BBC World Service broadcast I have just heard, a coup is imminent; if it's true, you may not get mail for some time. Don't worry! It won't involve me.

The 22nd and the 23rd passed without incident but, on the morning of the 24th, I awoke to find that there was nothing but martial music on all the radio stations. (I confess I actually found it a pleasant change from the relentless tango music which I never did find a good way to start the day, although it's deeply exciting in a dark cellar bar at night.) It had happened.

Initially, hopes were high. Terrorist outrages decreased dramatically. Universally, people began behaving more responsibly. The streets were cleaned, the lights worked, shops opened, airmail letters from home arrived only two days after posting, rather than the usual week to ten days, and trains ran punctually. As far as I was concerned, the coup was a welcome event.

So I had every confidence that the train timetabled to get me back to college in time for my duty would not fail to do so that day, but when it stopped at Avellaneda, on the way to Quilmes, just after passing over the Riachuelo, masses of armed troops rushed out of the station and surrounded us.

There was lots of shouting and the sound of running army boots. All the passengers were ordered off the train and herded into the station building with much pushing and shoving by the troops as they swarmed through the train, using their guns to poke people who didn't move sufficiently quickly. Officers shouted at the soldiers and the soldiers, in turn, shouted at the passengers. Several people fell down in the panic. There was a great deal of screaming and calling as people tried to locate their husbands, wives, children and friends separated in the melee.

A whisper went around that there were terrorists on the train. This was despite the order for silence and the waving of sub-machine guns, which was designed to intimidate and create fear among the guilty and innocent alike. There was a great deal of upset, sobbing and supplication for divine intervention. Crucifixes and rosaries were plainly visible in many hands.

We were divided into groups of about thirty, placed in separate rooms and made to stand with our backs against the walls. Six soldiers, with automatic weapons apparently at the ready, stood back to back in the centre of the room in which I was installed. We were ordered to remove our coats and jackets so that we could be searched easily. We were all anxious. I could see perspiration glistening on foreheads. Under the arms of the soldiers and the passengers, large, dark, damp patches demonstrated our collective fear. Every few seconds I could feel drips of sweat running down my own body in that hot, airless, frightened room.

The soldiers were mostly very young conscripts, who didn't even look as old as the college prefects, and they were certainly afraid; their eyes flitted from the passengers to each other as though looking for reassurance. They held their guns against their shoulders, aimed at the chests and heads of the five or six passengers immediately in front of them. Silence settled on the room. Although I tried to keep my eyes down and away from the faces of the soldiers, aware that eye contact might be seen as defiance or provocation, I still found my gaze drifting up, curious to see where others were looking and what the soldiers were doing. I could see the guns. Looking directly down the black hole of a gun barrel is a gut-wrenching experience. Fingers appeared to be on the triggers, but I couldn't tell if safety catches were on. It occurred to me that I'd never know if a trigger was squeezed when a gun was pointing at me. Oblivion. How hard would that be for my parents? And what about Juan Salvado? Who else would look after him properly? No, I had to get through this for their sakes. All I had to do was look at the floor and do as I was told.

One by one we were searched. Each of us in turn was made to take a couple of paces forward while soldiers looked, I assumed, for concealed weapons. The inspection was carried out in an intimate and unnecessarily brutal way. No consideration was given to privacy or to the fact that young men were searching both men and women of all ages. But, of course, no one protested. Within an hour or so everyone had been searched

130

and had their papers checked. We were ordered back on to the train and allowed to depart, much to the great relief of everybody. Word went round that some people had been taken away. I had no idea whether that was true or not. All I knew was that looking down the barrels of half a dozen machine guns held by young and nervous conscripts was a very scary experience. I'd had no confidence that the soldiers or the officers were doing their jobs properly. I wondered then if Argentina had jumped out of the frying pan and into the fire . . .

'Motorbikes are definitely not compatible
with explorers who have penguins as
travelling companions.'

12

The Mascot

In which Juan Salvador saves the day

At the start of each new term, all the boys were generally fit and well, but after a while an 'off-games' notice began to circulate listing boys with illnesses and injuries. Such youngsters were still expected to get out for fresh air and exercise, if they could. Depending on the severity of their affliction, they would be encouraged to take a gentle turn around the games fields or a more energetic walk down to the river.

It wasn't long before a small group of 'off-games' students came to ask if they could take Juan Salvado with them as they exercised around the fields while the other boys were playing rugby, and so it was that Juan Salvado was introduced to that 'game for hooligans that is played by gentlemen'.

The particular match they took him to see was between two under-fourteen teams — a match I was refereeing. Juan Salvado stayed with his little group of minders as they moved up and down the touchline offering encouragement and advice to their friends, such as, 'Get stuck in, you lazy slob,' and other helpful comments.

For what reason Juan Salvado always stayed on his side of the touchline and remained close

133

to his companions, I cannot say. The fact remains that he attended many rugby games with different minders and although he would rush up and down the touchline, keeping close to the play as though keen to miss none of the action, never did he encroach on to the pitch or get too close. If a sudden change of play caused a rush of players to bear down on him, willing hands would snatch him from the ground and move him to safety.

Of course, it didn't take long for the under-fourteen team to realize that a penguin was precisely the sort of macho mascot that a fearless rugby team needed to strike fear and dread into any opposition. So Juan Salvado became the official team talisman and doubtless brought luck to his adoptive players. (Or perhaps that should be 'adopted', for I am really not sure who adopted whom.)

One warm and balmy Thursday afternoon, not long after, I was at the end of refereeing a 'possibles' vs 'probables' practice game in preparation for an important match, under the careful gaze of our mascot, when a chilling message arrived.

In those days telephone calls, like international air travel, were extremely expensive. To get an idea of relative values, you have to understand that the London-Buenos Aires return flight on a BOAC VC10 (magnificent aircraft though it was) cost more than £1,000 at a time when the average income was about £50 a week.

International phone calls were not simply an

indulgence, they were prohibitively expensive — maybe fifty or a hundred times their cost now — and personal calls were only made in dire circumstances. This wasn't a terrible inconvenience; airmail letters took no more than a week on average to arrive at their destination, but could take as little as two days if one happened to catch the post 'just right'. They were also cheap to send — just pennies. Dutifully, I wrote home at least once a week, and was a good correspondent with other friends and relations, too. Following the unexpected arrival of Juan Salvado, my missives had actually acquired some genuinely interesting news for those at home. The pleasure of writing and receiving a handwritten letter shouldn't be underestimated; however, there were no phone calls at all, until that particular afternoon.

A wavering voice came running on weary legs across the fields, calling for me: 'Mrs Trent's compliments and there's an international phone call for you!' The message came via a relay of runners to reach me, conveniently situated at the furthest end of the campus, at least half a mile from the office. I looked towards the boys with Juan Salvado and indicated that they should take him back to the terrace and not wait for me.

There were two types of service level for international phone calls. Phoning 'place to place' was the cheaper option; the call was charged per minute for the entire time the call was connected. The alternative, 'person to person', was twice the price, but the charges didn't start until the required person arrived at the handset and

135

was able to talk to the caller. If, for any reason, the intended recipient was unavailable, then there was no charge.

I could only surmise that something unpleasant had happened. It was the only possible reason anyone would make an international phone call. After all, 'no news was good news', wasn't it? Obviously, someone had died. The possibilities flashed through my mind. Grandparents were in their eighties. They had been well when I left home. Parents were in their sixties. They hadn't said anything was amiss in their letters. Siblings or other close friends perhaps? That seemed unlikely. It's moments like that when you realize you actually have a preference about these things. Oh, please don't let it be . . . An icy anxiety gripped me and I felt the blood drain from my face as a cold perspiration, which had nothing to do with the exertion of the game, formed on my brow. I battled to maintain the appearance of composure.

Running to get there quickly, but walking at intervals to make sure I had enough breath to be able to respond when I arrived, I made my way to the admin office.

Whom would I fly home for? What a hideous question to have to answer. I had money in the bank to get home in an emergency, but not for a return flight. I had been living in Argentina for less than a year and hadn't begun to slake my wanderlust. Oh, what an unkind turn of fate! The single flight home would be equivalent to the cost of a family car now. I couldn't be expected to pay that for some distant relative I might never have met, could I? But there would be no question if . . . Oh, please don't let it be . . .

My heart was hammering as I got to the office. I kicked off my muddy boots and went in. Sarah gave me a kind, concerned smile. She was the college secretary, a truly sympathetic, helpful lady who was relied upon by the young ex-pats who needed a bit of TLC from time to time.

The receiver was lying on her desk next to the base. It was black and ominous and I hated it for the pain it was about to bring me. She picked it up and put her hand over the mouthpiece.

'It's person to person, so don't rush. Just wait till you've got your breath back. Take a few deep breaths,' she whispered to me.

To the international operator she lied, 'I can see him coming now. He'll be here in a couple of minutes.'

She put the phone down as she walked round the desk, giving me a wan smile. She touched my forearm momentarily with her fingers. 'Be strong' was the message. Then she walked out of the office, shutting the door firmly to allow me some privacy.

I took a deep breath, picked up the phone and said 'Hello' as steadily as I could.

'Hello. This is the International Operator. I have a person to person call for Tom Michell from his mother. Are you he?' piped a thin voice, seemingly from a great distance.

Mother calling . . . so that meant . . . I felt devastated — the foundation of my world was about to fall apart. My gut tightened. I knew . . .

I spoke in a semi-shout to the faint, far-away voice.

'I am,' I said.

'Putting you through now, caller,' she said.

'Hello, Mother?'

'Hello . . . is that you, Tom? Can you hear me, Tom?'

'Yes, can you speak up? I can hardly hear you.'

'IS THAT BETTER? CAN YOU HEAR ME NOW?'

'YES, I CAN.'

'OH, HELLO, DARLING! HAPPY BIRTH-DAY!'

'WHAT?!!'

'Happy Birthday, darling! I'm phoning to say Happy Birthday!'

Churning emotions choked me. Was it my birthday? It was. Was that really all she was phoning for? Everyone was alive and well!

We spoke briefly and I dissembled as I struggled to get my thoughts and words back from grieving gravesides to birthday balloons, desperately endeavouring to sound pleased to hear from her. I didn't want to admit what a fright her unexpected call had given me, but she didn't appear to be listening to what I was saying.

Suddenly she cut me short. 'But how is that poor little penguin? I've been so worried about him. Is he getting enough to eat do you think?' I did my best to assuage her doubts about my penguin husbandry. 'Well, I just had to know that Juan Salvado is all right. Now, I must go for a walk with the dogs; your father will have a fit when he sees the phone bill; make sure you look after my dear little penguin properly! I've told everybody about him!'

'Is everything all right?' asked Sarah after I had hung up and opened the door, but volunteered nothing. 'I've made you some tea. I thought it might have been bad news . . . ' She studied my face, searching for clues, ready to give me a supportive hug if that was what I needed.

'You're very kind,' I said. 'It's nothing bad. Just Mother phoning to say 'Happy Birthday'. I had completely forgotten! At least, I think that's why she phoned. She might have been phoning to make sure I was looking after Juan Salvado properly!' We looked at each other for several moments until our stony expressions melted and we laughed. If there were tears in my eyes they were tears of laughter. All was right with the world. I staggered out of the office like a drunk; my muscles had turned to jelly.

The zenith of the rugby season and the local derby was the match against arch-rivals St Boniface. These were needle matches and no quarter was given, ever. The fixture was always the last of the season because the two were generally considered to be the best rugby schools in Buenos Aires.

The day of the St Boniface match was always a

social occasion. The host school alternated each year and each of the five school years put forward a team. The St Boniface Match Saturdays were special. Morning school ended earlier than usual, which allowed for a light lunch before the games to be followed by a sumptuous and convivial *asado* — a colossal Argentine barbecue — for everyone involved afterwards.

Because the rivalry was so fierce, external referees always officiated and everything was done to try to ensure that the Corinthian Spirit was upheld. The missed morning lessons also allowed the junior matches to start about forty-five minutes before the 1st XV game so that the younger players could watch and support the climax of the senior competition.

In the preceding weeks, all of St George's daily practice games had been focussed on having a team in the peak of fitness while skills and moves were rehearsed until every player knew precisely what was expected. Training with weights and sprints on the running track were combined with tactics on the field conducted with military precision, while strategy was rigorously explained in classrooms where there were blackboards to describe manoeuvres from the perspective of a flying bird's eye. Nothing was left to chance. The headmaster himself always made a point of attending for some part of every sporting match through the year, and nobody doubted the significance of the results to the prestige of the college. As the all-important St Boniface fixture drew closer, the headmaster even started attending practices, and the senior rugby coaching staff gave up their free time to help advise the juniors. Juan Salvado's afternoon walks allowed him to see for himself the progress each team was making.

Rugby was not played by all schools in Buenos Aires so many of the boys knew their opposing contemporaries quite well. Accordingly, each team had a fair idea of the strengths and weaknesses of their opponents and, of course, results of other inter-school matches were a matter of record.

At the under-fourteen level, St Boniface had one particularly able player. He was known to be their match winner. He was fearless in tackles and was the fastest hundred-metre sprinter of his age in the province. It seemed a trifle unsporting that his name was Walker.

Walker played in the full-back position and his defence was so secure that the other fourteen team members could concentrate fully on attacking because of the confidence he inspired in them. But such was the boy's ability in reading the game that he was sometimes able to join in the attack at key moments and so provide an extra overlapping player. If Walker got the ball in his hands, a try was almost certainly scored. He had been playing the game since starting mini-rugby at the age of six or seven and he had captained his side on almost every occasion since the boys had started playing competitive games.

Luis Fernández was captain of the St George's under-fourteen team. He was a big lad and strong for his age and he took his responsibilities seriously, but his rugby was pedestrian by comparison with Walker's. From the kick-off there was tension in the air, but it soon settled down to a

141

simple hard slog with both teams trying to win possession of the ball. Each side was battling for control and fighting hard to execute a plan for scoring; meanwhile the opposing team was doing its level best to spoil those endeavours.

The game ebbed and flowed and there wasn't much in it. The spectators felt that the superior side was St Boniface. St George's made the first bad mistake, just before half-time. From a scrappy piece of play the ball emerged to St George's advantage, and it was seized by one of our forwards who attempted to clear it with a long flat pass to the backs. However, it was too close to our goal line and our players were not well positioned. Walker read the situation immaculately. From ten yards out he sprinted like the wind and intercepted the ball in mid-flight between passer and recipient. Taken at full speed, he ran past the dismayed St George's players, who were either standing still or running in the wrong direction, powerless to stop him. In only a couple of seconds Walker had touched the ball down and scored the first try of the game, close to the touchline, and put St Boniface 4 points (in those days) ahead. Luckily, their kicker was unable to send the ball over the bar from such a difficult angle and thus failed to add another two points.

When the referee's whistle blew at half-time the score stood at 4 — 0 to St Boniface, and players from both sides retired to their respective ends of the field to discuss the game with their coaches. In the days before advertisers started telling people that it was imperative to drink water every few minutes from plastic bottles, expensively imported over very large distances, players at all levels were able to survive for the full seventy or eighty minutes of a rugby game with nothing more than a quarter of an orange to recharge their systems in the interval. The bearer of this refreshment was accompanied by the off-games boys, who, of course, had brought Juan Salvado in support of their peers. After words of wisdom and encouragement had been delivered by the coaches, team players moved to deposit their orange rinds in a bucket and, as they did so, stooped to stroke the head of the penguin mascot for good luck. Juan Salvado tried to avoid these liberties by running off in a different direction from the one he was facing, a feat made possible by his panoramic vision. As the players took to the field again he preened himself, as usual pausing every few seconds to look around and vigorously flap his wings, examine his feathers, shake his head and occasionally walk between the boys' legs.

After a five-minute break, play resumed in the warm afternoon sunshine. Juan Salvado was taken by his custodians to the safest place on the field, the opponents' end, beyond the goalposts. All St Boniface had to do to win was prevent St George's from scoring. On the other hand, St George's needed to score twice to claim victory. Nobody was rating the chances of the home side very highly.

Walker commanded his troops with the cool reassurance that came only from exceptional skills and experience. His teammates willingly accepted his orders. From his position at the back of the field he had the vantage point of a general. Fernández was a far less experienced player. The contrast was stark. The calm, relaxed Walker was in complete control of both his game and his emotions, while Fernández, though doing his absolute best to secure a win, was red in the face and exhausted, sweat drenching his hair and running down his face. He had been trying to be everywhere at once, yelling encouragement and instructions to his team while fighting for all he was worth to win possession of the ball. Minutes ticked by and the play remained stubbornly in St George's half, a sure sign that St Boniface was the better team. Everyone felt certain that if St Boniface scored a second try, it would undoubtedly seal the match for them.

As the game entered its closing minutes and the spectators, believing this game was lost, were beginning to drift away to watch the 1st XV match, which was well under way, everything changed. Play had moved to the centre of the field and St George's forwards suddenly got control of the ball. The scrum-half picked it up and made a good linking pass to the backs, who started to run with it. Our opponents marked them well and tackled man for man.

Walker stood calmly near his goal line watching the game unfold. He wasn't concerned. He had a defender in place for every St George's attacker. Meanwhile Fernández was struggling to his feet and sprinting to assist. He screamed for the ball, which was passed to him. Suddenly in those closing seconds it had all come down to this encounter, a simple dual between the two captains.

Walker smiled. He knew he was the better player. All the other players had stopped moving to watch the drama. Fernández yelled for support and Walker's smile widened as he saw a new opportunity opening for him. Fernández would either have to make a very long pass or face a tackle by Walker. If he chose to pass the ball, Walker would have a good chance of intercepting it, as he had done earlier in the game, and scoring a second try. If Fernández didn't pass at all, Walker would simply tackle him, the ball would fall to the ground, go out of play and St Boniface would triumph.

Fernández prepared for the long pass and, glancing to gauge the position of the vice-captain who was belatedly running in support, he swung his arms wide to the left to make an enormous pass to the right. With all his might he ripped his arms across his body in an attempt to power the ball to his teammate. Walker ran to intercept it, his timing cat-like in its perfection, but he realized too late that Fernández hadn't actually released the ball! He had dummied a pass and Walker had fallen for a simple trick.

The momentum of the feigned pass changed Fernández's path and after a few paces he hammered the ball to the ground, scoring a try right under the posts for St George's. Four points all! The referee blew the whistle.

'Yes!' shouted Fernández. 'Yes! Just like Juan Salvado! I looked one way and ran the other!' and the rest of his words were lost in cheering and applause. Juan Salvado was flapping his wings in wild applause too, and beaming at

145

everyone as he accepted their acclaim for his contribution to the dramatic improvement in our fortunes. Occasionally he stopped and shook his head vigorously, in a self-deprecating sort of way, just as an orchestra's conductor attempts to deflect some of the plaudits back on to the musicians.

A hush descended as the St George's kicker prepared for the most important conversion of his life. Directly in front of the posts, all he had to do was get the ball over the crossbar to be awarded two more points and win the game. He placed the ball, took three paces back, lowered his head, lined up the ball with the posts, paused, breathed deeply, accelerated and struck it. The ball flew straight and true. The referee blew his final whistle to end the game and another great cheer went up from the home-side supporters. Victory by six points to four!

The captains shook hands with each other, sportsmanlike to the very end, then with the referee and finally with the coaches of the opposing teams, and Juan Salvado returned to his terrace to take a well-earned rest. But as everyone left the field, Walker was heard to remark to his father that he thought the St Boniface coaches could learn some lessons from the penguin.

13

A Visit to Maria's House

*In which Juan Salvador's circle of
admirers grows larger*

I planned to leave for Peninsula Valdés — to investigate the possibility and practicality of releasing Juan Salvado in the penguin colonies there — during the week-long half-term. Maria, assisted by the prefects, had tended Juan Salvado enthusiastically when I had been out of college overnight from time to time, so I thought I'd ask her first if she would look after him while I was away. Her smile when I did confirmed that I hadn't asked too much. There were various poultry sheds at her house, she said, and some would be vacant, so it was arranged that we'd accompany her home after work on the day before I was due to depart on my reconnaissance trip.

Maria lived a short walk from the college. After her husband had died she'd gone to live with her brother in the house where she was born, helping with domestic chores, just as she had when she was a child. As well as preparing food in the kitchen, she'd feed the hens and pigs, wash and mend clothes, mind the little children when their mothers were out at work and pump water from the well: all the things required by a large extended family.

Juan Salvado and I met Maria as she emerged from her sewing room at the appointed time and we set off for her house with a supply of fish I had brought with me. We were in no hurry — indeed, Maria never hurried. At Maria's pace Juan Salvado had no difficulty in keeping up and my companions walked at ease, their identical rolling gait reminding me of a pair of metronomes.

I learned from Maria that in her father's day land had been given to families who were prepared to work the soil and make their living from its upkeep. Land on the river side of town, which was poor and stony, had been marked off in hundred-metre squares and long ago Maria's father had been a grateful recipient. He had built a house of wood, initially with only one room. Working as a journeyman, getting a day's labour when he could, and working at home when he couldn't find paid employment, he had raised his family. I think Maria told me there were eleven of them living there at one stage. The older boys eventually left to make their own way in the world, with nothing more than the clothes they stood up in, and the girls had married boys from similar families and gone to start the cycle again.

'What are your earliest memories, Maria?' I asked. I had discovered that older people loved talking about the world they remembered and a cornucopia of wonders invariably opened up.

'Oh, simple things. Collecting eggs from the hens in the morning to make breakfast. How cool and dark it was inside the house and how hot and bright the sun was outside. I remember

148

how pretty my mother was and how strong my father was and the squeak of the gate and the water pump. I remember being taken to see the first trains at Quilmes station. I had never imagined anything could be so big and powerful and noisy. I was frightened almost to death! I remember seeing the first cars in Quilmes too. You had to be enormously rich to own a car in those days!'

'I wish I could afford a car,' I said with no little chagrin, thinking of my own, sitting on blocks and parked under dust sheets in England. 'It would make everything so much easier going to Valdés! Have you ever wanted a car, Maria?'

She was astonished that such a thought had occurred to me.

'Gracious heavens, no! No, not for a moment! What should I do with a car?' She laughed. 'I only want things that make me happy. So many people are captivated by things that can never make them happy!'

'What makes you happy, then, Maria?'

'Oh, my children and my family make me happy, and my friends. Growing things makes me happy. Flowers on the tomatoes and the swelling fruit. The hens, the pigs and the goats make me happy. My work makes me happy, too.' She paused and then said, 'Growing older with the people I love makes me happy.'

I considered this profound statement for a moment and then asked, 'Do penguins make you happy, Maria?' and looked at Juan Salvado, walking along with us, drinking in the conversation.

She laughed out loud. 'Oh, yes, penguins make me very happy,' she said and Juan Salvado looked up suddenly to see what we were laughing at. 'Of course penguins make me happy! Who wouldn't be happy walking along this dusty track with a penguin in the late afternoon?' Juan Salvado beamed at us.

After that we walked in silence for a while and I watched Juan Salvado as we ambled along. He looked around him all the time, at the path, at the plants, at the fences and at us.

The walk to Maria's house took about half an hour at our casual pace, and when we arrived, I was delighted to see a mixture of small buildings and enclosures, trees and bushes, patches of cultivated ground and others left fallow. It seemed to be the very place to provide shelter and interest for Juan Salvado.

But at that moment, from out of the sun, a huge, wolf-sized, rabid dog leaped over a wall and came racing towards us. Its ears were laid flat on its head and its red frothing tongue showed between bared white teeth and contrasted with the evil in its eyes. It kicked up clouds of dust as it accelerated over the few yards that separated us. For a second I hesitated, unsure whether to defend Juan Salvado by lifting him out of the dog's reach or by attacking the dog directly. But even as I wavered it became clear that its intended victim wasn't Juan Salvado, but Maria herself. Before I had any time to react it hit her in the solar plexus and drove all the wind out of her body so that she staggered backwards and was forced to grasp at the dog's head in order to keep her balance. I was astounded that she wasn't knocked clean off her feet. The dog had its head buried deep into Maria's middle in a frenzied attack and its flailing tail seemed to keep driving it forward, like a propeller.

'Oooooofff!' exhaled Maria on the impact.

Too stunned by the speed of the attack, I stood in stupefied horror until I realized Maria was actually fondling the dog's ears. 'Oh, you silly dog, Reno, yes, I'm home, now get off.'

Juan Salvado, meanwhile, was quite unperturbed by the dramatic appearance of the hound, which was clearly a South American relation of that belonging to Baskerville, and continued sniffing some wayside buttercups that had caught his attention.

'Reno!' A man's voice came from the other side of the wall and the dog retreated as quickly as it had appeared, back the way it had come.

'Maria!' I said, still feeling my muscles shaking. 'I thought that dog was going to attack you!'

'Oh, he's just a boisterous puppy, he'll calm down soon enough,' she said as she rearranged her coat and recovered her breath, 'but it would be an error for anyone to enter my brother's property uninvited. Come and meet him. Ah! He's here now.'

An unoiled gate squeaked and was held open for us by a stocky, swarthy man, well advanced in years. His still-powerful frame spoke of a lifetime of labour and his twinkling eyes matched his smile.

Inside the gate he shook my hand and said, 'Welcome to our home, señor. I am Mano. I hope you weren't alarmed by Reno — sometimes people are, you know, but he wouldn't harm a fly, would you, boy?' and the dog's tail stirred up a cloud of dust as he wagged it even faster. Reno was lying on the ground at his master's heel, head erect and at attention. His tongue lolled out of his mouth as he panted, more in restraint than in recovery, awaiting a command. One of his eyes was green, the other brown, and both were watching me intently. There was something about that dog's demeanour which suggested he was laughing at me.

'Ah! And this must be Juan Salvado,' Mano continued, making a deep bow and looking at the penguin who was walking forward as he examined the unfamiliar surroundings. 'You're both most welcome. Come in now and we'll have something to drink. Nola! Our guests are here! Reno, bed! Mateo! Donna, Gloria! Where are you, grandchildren? Come and see our guests! Come!'

No sooner had these commands been given and we had started walking towards the house, than a woman, whom I took to be Nola, approached with a large tray of mixed refreshments, and young children appeared from different directions. One of the girls was clutching a nervous-looking white rabbit while the boy whittled a stick with his penknife. Reno instantly ran towards the house and into a wooden kennel.

Mano turned and led the way to a corner of the courtyard in front of the house, which was

152

shaded by an ancient bougainvillea creeper with many purple bracts surrounding the little white flowers, which had been trained to grow through a wooden frame supported by poles.

Mano sat in a chair, which was clearly his, and motioned me to another. 'Would you like a drink?' he asked. 'I myself will have *mate* now. Do you like *mate*?' But before I could say that the Argentine tea (pronounced ma-tay) reminded me of nothing so much as an infusion of dried grass taken from a field too recently grazed by cattle, he had ordered Nola to bring some more, a command which she had already anticipated and carried out. As she passed she offered to put the fish I had brought into the fridge but brought a few back on a plate, so I could show the children how to feed Juan Salvado.

And so began a delightful interlude in which this charming, extraordinary and exasperating man ordered the people around him to do things they had already done and kept up a continuous commentary about things everybody could see perfectly well for themselves.

'Donna, put the fish in the fridge. Quickly, girl, before it goes bad.'

'Maria, get another cushion for the señor, he needs another cushion.'

'Mateo, where is your brother Ernesto? Tell him to come here at once, I need him.'

'Donna! Where are you, girl? Never where you should be. Here, girl. Go and tell the neighbours to come and meet the señor and Juan Salvado the penguin.'

'Gloria, get some fish and feed the penguin.

153

He must be tired after such a long walk. I want to see him eating.' (Nola had already put a few sprats on a dish and placed them beside me.)

'Good, here you are at last, Ernesto, go and get some more chairs.' (This to a young man as he appeared, staggering beneath armfuls of chairs which he then set about arranging for a large party of people.)

'Nola! Come here, woman! Come and look at this penguin, he is such a handsome bird, don't you think? Look at him scratching his head with his foot! Did you know, Maria, that the señor found him in Brazil and brought him home? Nola! Where are you?'

'Now, Ernesto, I want you to put the chairs around for lots of people to sit down. Ernesto!'

'Ah! There you are, Nicolás and Martina. Welcome, neighbours, come and look at this wonderful penguin. Look, he can scratch his head with his foot. Did you ever see the like? Sit down there, good.'

'Ha, ha, ha! Look at the penguin! Martina, go inside and get some of the fish from the fridge. I want to see the penguin eating some fish, don't you, Nicolás?'

'What's that rabbit doing here? Take it away, girl!'

'Ah! You're back at last, Mia, whatever took you so long? Never mind that now! Come and look at this penguin!'

'Martina! Have you found the fish? Maria, go and show Martina where Donna has put the fish.'

I pushed the dish over towards him.

'Oh! Here they are, everybody, I've found them! Now come here, all of you, and look at this! Juan Salvado is going to eat some fish! I'm going to feed him. Have you ever seen a penguin before, neighbour? Look how he can scratch his head!'

And so he picked up a fish and held it out. Juan Salvado stood patiently for the fish to be dangled within his reach, but Mano's attention was taken by the next event, so penguin and fish remained about a foot apart.

'Look, everybody, Joaquín's just arrived. Did you get all that done? Just as I told you, Joaquín? No problems I hope? Come and look at this penguin, Joaquín. He was rescued, you know, and now he is going to stay with us for a few days. Now, I have some wire, I want you to make sure that the old chicken run is secure for him. Oh! Where is the wire? Maria! Where did I put that wire? Aggghhh!'

At that very moment Juan Salvado snatched the fish from Mano's hand and almost took his fingers too; his arm had slowly been descending while he was talking and once the fish was in range, Juan Salvado didn't stand on ceremony. The fish was gone with the familiar resounding clack. Mano's hand shot up. 'Oh!' he said, checking his fingers. 'Did you see that? Come and look at this, everybody! Look how quickly the penguin eats the fish. Oh, I've never seen anything like it! Gloria, child, come here, you can be next to give the penguin a fish. Do it as I have just shown you. Well go on, girl, it won't hurt you.'

155

Gloria took a deep breath, picked up a fish and bravely held it out for Juan Salvado in a much more considerate way, quite unlike Mano's demonstration.

And so Mano kept up his running commentary. More and more people kept arriving, friends, relations and neighbours, and I quickly lost track of his careful introductions. They sat on chairs or on the ground, drinking *mate* in a semi-circle around Juan Salvado who, as always, loved being the centre of attention, and did everything he could to steal the lime-light from Mano. He preened his feathers and ate fish to the great appreciation of his audience, who watched spellbound.

Juan Salvado appeared to be totally content, as always, in appreciative company so it was easy for me to make my apologies to Maria and to leave unnoticed to set off for my trip to visit wild penguins, completely happy that she and the others would look after him over the four or five days I would be away.

'But will it hatch?'

14

Going Wild for Penguins

*In which I visit colonies of penguins and
have close encounters with other wildlife*

The next day arrived and with it my long-promised
expedition to Peninsula Valdés. I had worked
tirelessly to get everything prepared in order to
leave Buenos Aires as soon as I could get away. I
had a folder full of papers, each authenticated
by a local notary public to show that I was the
legal owner of the bike, and I had another set of
papers to validate the bona fides of those nota-
ries. Interestingly, none of the papers I was required
to obtain concerned the road-worthiness of the
machine.

In the college workshops I had carefully crafted
two pannier boxes for the motorcycle from ply-
wood and angle aluminium, designed to carry
the two spare tyres I was going to take as part
of the all-inclusive toolkit for nursing the 200cc
Gilera through the expedition. By uncompromis-
ing determination I had been able to pack spare
fuel and oil, a tent and sleeping bag, an alcohol
stove and minuscule rations, together with one
change of clothes and a pocket-size first-aid kit. I
was going to rough it, live wild!

And so I had taken the motorbike by train
to Bahía Blanca. Rail travel was marvellously

cheap, just a few pesos per mile. It wasn't quick and the distances were immense, but it meant I could cover the first five hundred odd miles in less than a day. I had to travel with the bike in the guard's van along with everything I'd brought with me, for I couldn't be sure it would be safe if I left it unattended.

Argentina is blessed with a long and spectacular coastline, parts of which are notable breeding grounds for maritime birds and animals. Peninsula Valdés, which lies some 900 miles by road from St George's, is one such, renowned not only for colonies of penguins but also for sea lions, elephant seals and whales. Situated on the north-eastern corner of the southern province of Chubut, which is larger than England and Scotland combined, the peninsula is almost an island, being connected to the mainland only by the narrowest isthmus. The area of Peninsula Valdés is almost exactly the same size as that of Cornwall or Long Island and resembles, as much as it resembles anything, the shape of an embryonic penguin joined to the mainland by an umbilical cord. In consequence there are two large gulfs of very sheltered water, with a total area equal to that of the 'island'. This combination of ocean currents, latitude and topography has produced a very desirable location for pelagic birds and mammals to assemble annually. Even today, the total human population of the entire province of Chubut is no larger than that of Cornwall (some half a

159

million). Here one can find peace and solitude, another reason why its wildlife is so rich, and even before I had met Juan Salvado I had wished to explore this wild and wonderful region.

I was aware that I was vulnerable to many perils, travelling alone in such an isolated place. In those days many Argentines who could afford it had bodyguards and guns were legal, available and inexpensive, so many travellers carried them even if they didn't like to admit it. I had often considered buying a firearm but was uncertain if it really made for safety.

I had navigated south from Bahía Blanca along the coast to San Antonio and on to the peninsula. The bike performed astonishingly well and I made excellent progress. I filled my fuel cans at every opportunity and enquired about the distance to the next supply. I found my own fuel at little roadside eateries and replenished my supplies so that I always had just sufficient food for a couple of days.

The geology of Valdés is stunning — low lying and semidesert — but this made the contrast of the rich wildlife all the more exceptional. The roads were all unmetalled and clouds of dust rose behind me. From the high ground I could see long curving beaches and the ocean stretching out beyond. Areas of sparse vegetation made it easy to take the bike off-road and I made little detours to get better views. In my ebullience, I had imagined penguins would be easy to find, if not positively flocking out to greet me in the way Juan Salvado did every morning on the terrace. Instead, on the beaches along the coast of the peninsula I saw pinnipeds — elephant seals, sea lions and seals — gathered in great profusion for the mating season, and to have their young.

Adult male South American sea lions are magnificent animals, and well-named. Having quite a short muzzle, a huge head and shoulders with a magnificent mane of orange-brown fur, they are really quite leonine. Gathered on the beach defending their territories and their harems, they would raise their noses as high as they could in order to dominate rivals.

The popularity of the waters around Valdés with these creatures made them rich hunting grounds for the killer whales that circled offshore, but I witnessed these remarkable sea lions leap from the water and clamber steep inclines to access the sanctuary of the many plateaux, a feature of the Valdés coastline. Somehow the adults were able to get a purchase on those craggy slopes and so snatch defenceless cubs from the water and lift them to safety by the scruffs of their necks.

There were no barriers at this time separating the wildlife from tourists like me, but discretion ensured that I never approached one closer than about thirty yards. At that range they rolled their heads sideways, sucked in their cheeks and looked at me with damp, twinkling eyes. It was a gesture I decided to respect.

Sea elephant bulls are even bigger than sea lions, much, much bigger, and much uglier,

161

having a pendulous protuberance like a large crumpled boot where they could reasonably expect to have a nose. An adult male of this leviathan species can exceed twenty feet in length and four tons in weight — more than twice the length and ten times the weight of a sea lion — and even thirty yards didn't seem an adequate safety margin, although they are far less agile on land than sea lions and managed to make the latter seem the epitome of grace.

Everywhere I looked I was transfixed by duels of shocking violence, as great bulls of each species fought for local dominance. One grim battle ended with the loser being hurled down a precipice. Combatants reared up and fell, like trees, on to their adversaries, slashing, biting and ripping flesh in the process, oblivious to the cows and calves around. The air echoed with these encounters and the very beach seemed to shake and the wounds of both victor and vanquished were terrible to see. I wasn't surprised that I didn't locate any penguins near these territories.

Further from the coast, grasslands and scrubby flora were home to ñandú or rhea, an ostrich-like flightless bird standing some four foot six inches high, and guanaco, a deer-like relative of the camel. Being considerably taller than the vegetation, both were very conspicuous and were wary of me if I approached them too closely, but would regard me with only passing interest as I rode past on the dirt tracks.

On this, my first visit to Valdés, I didn't see another human being for the whole time I was there. Neither did I see a penguin, despite searching for nearly two whole days. I put the latter issue down to lack of local knowledge and a coastline of several hundred miles, so with intelligence of the existence of other colonies further south, I decided to cut my losses. The following day I made my way to Punta Tombo, where I had been told I would be certain to find penguins in what was apparently a favourite breeding ground.

At some point during the ride to Punta Tombo I knew for certain that a storm was brewing. The temperature had dropped, the sky had darkened, the wind had changed direction and its strength had increased considerably. Riding a motorbike in very heavy rain on dirt roads is impossible, but being caught out in a hailstorm on the pampas can be dangerous — even fatal — because the hailstones can grow extremely large. Immediately, I looked for a stand of trees that would afford protection from the rain which I expected at any minute. At the next track, I turned off the road and took shelter under the largest of six or so eucalyptus trees in a spinney. The noise as the storm started was quite unexpected. Initially, the hailstones were small, no bigger than raisins, and rattled through the trees, but with the storm's growing intensity came an increase in their size. By the time it reached its zenith they were as big as golf balls or chicken eggs, crashing through the trees, ripping off leaves and twigs, and bouncing and clattering all around with a deafening noise. In free fall, hailstones like these can do real damage to glass, cars, livestock and people; I had been told that hailstones had been known to reach the size of croquet balls and could kill cattle. I kept my motorcycle helmet on and sheltered as best I could in the lee of a tree, so avoiding almost all of them. Eventually, the storm subsided, but it was still impossible to continue because the road remained covered with ice. There was nothing to be done but wait until it melted. I thought about Juan Salvado taking cover beneath his table on the terrace and assumed the penguins here would seek sanctuary in the water when they found themselves assailed by cannonballs of ice.

The minor road that led to Punta Tombo was a simple pot-holed dirt track, so the hundred or so miles from the Valdés Peninsula to the point took a full day, but when I eventually arrived, the sight was so breathtaking, so spectacular, so abounding with Magellan penguins, that I knew it would have been worth it even if I'd had to push the bike the entire way.

All around and along the coast to the north were penguins in uncountable numbers. Whereas Valdés would take months to explore thoroughly, Punta Tombo is a peninsula only two miles long. What made this little location so much more desirable to penguins was unclear to me — perhaps it really was the absence of pinnipeds — but I had to believe that a million penguins couldn't be wrong about their choice. As I watched, every single bird was doing something that I had learned was characteristic behaviour of penguins.

There were penguins standing with their wings out like scarecrows and watching the other birds, heads constantly moving; there were penguins walking slowly; penguins running; penguins rushing into the water, swimming or climbing back out of the sea and calling to their mates; there were penguins marching determinedly up the beach to feed hungry chicks; penguins scratching their heads with their feet or rubbing their heads and necks against their chests and sides; penguins shaking their bottoms and penguins preening.

It would be wrong to dismiss 'preening' too quickly, because penguins spend so much time on this single activity. Using their beaks, penguins were preening their chests and their backs and their fronts. They were preening in front of their wings and behind their wings and under their wings and on top of their wings and along their wings, and over their shoulders and round their necks and round their legs and between their legs and under their bellies and round their tails and, indeed, every part of them that was accessible to their agile beaks. And for those feathers that weren't within reach of their beaks, they used their toes.

Thanks to Juan Salvado, I'd had the opportunity to study penguin feathers, to see they grow not at random points, but in rows and columns that together form a pattern round their bodies. I watched as, with faultless attention, each bird worked through every feather according to some formula of its own, just like Juan Salvado did every day, making sure that each one was in

165

perfect condition: waterproof, supple and sliding without a snag as it moved. Just as feathers have given birds mastery of the air so they have also allowed birds dominion of the earth's waters. Seeing this process close up made me understand just what a remarkable feat of evolutionary engineering feathers are; both feathers in general and penguin feathers in particular. I couldn't help but wonder at them. If penguins continue to evolve for another million years, is any further development possible? I couldn't see any possibility of improvement in performance.

But here at Punta Tombo I discovered something else, something I hadn't been able to learn by watching Juan Salvado. What I hadn't seen before was the familiarity of the birds and their involvement with each other. Many were parent birds tending their chicks, but even those that weren't appeared to communicate continually with other birds through eye contact. No single action of a penguin lasted for more than a few seconds, after which it would stop and look at its neighbours. Having apparently derived the necessary rest, reassurance or approval, the bird either continued with the action or started a new one. This was the social life of penguins and what Juan Salvado so obviously needed and found a substitute for in people. But I felt a real sadness for him, because humans are incapable of the continual interchange provided by penguin semaphore. I wondered how long I could have lived with penguins as my only company before I felt the need for human companionship, the equivalent to the condition Juan Salvado found himself in at St George's.

The ground around the beaches of Punta Tombo was riddled with holes and depressions in which penguins slept and nested. While some had only a few tail feathers hidden away, others were so deeply ensconced that only a beak tip was showing. These birds seemed to be the most inactive. They might have been sitting on eggs or chicks or staking a claim to the residence; I had no way of knowing and didn't want to disturb them by investigating more closely.

The penguins were not alone at Punta Tombo. There were small herds of guanaco wandering nearby with rabbits and occasional ñandús of varying ages and sizes. Although other species were often very close to the penguins, the contact was entirely peaceful and I didn't see any kind of interaction between them, except on one occasion. My attention was caught by an unusually excited group of penguins behaving quite differently from anything I'd seen so far. A little group of perhaps thirty birds had formed a tear-shaped phalanx that was in pursuit of some kind of prey. The leaders were lunging forward and pecking at their quarry, almost as though they were attempting a tackle. When the first rank fell, then the second rank of birds rushed past to form a new vanguard of attack, leaving the fallen penguins to rejoin the group from the rear. This progress continued for a distance of some fifty yards as other penguins watched the spectacle from a distance but made no attempt to join in.

I had no idea what the penguins were doing until I managed to glimpse their victim: an armadillo was scurrying away from the pecking beaks. It was making for the bushes, and only when it reached the sanctuary and protection afforded by the dense, thorny undergrowth did the determined pursuit of the penguins come to a halt. Had it been robbing eggs or chicks? I didn't know if that was part of the diet of these scaly creatures, but the penguins were not tolerating its presence in their colony and drove it out, only relinquishing their chase when the armadillo disappeared into the vegetation, impenetrable to all but the armoured animal. Having been the victim of a penguin peck myself, I felt for the interloper and rubbed my scarred finger, all too aware of its consternation.

Walking around the penguin colonies, there was little reaction from the birds unless I came too close. If I did, they simply moved out of the way so that I had a clear space all around me. They wouldn't let me get near enough to touch them or pick them up, but otherwise they seemed as indifferent to my presence as to that of the guanaco. When I sat on the ground they just continued about their business and ignored me as though I were not there at all. What a blissful moment that was, for I felt completely at one with the environment.

My time with these birds passed too quickly. I walked down the tiny peninsula and along the coast. Every little cove and flat piece of land was occupied, festooned with penguins. It wouldn't have been possible to cram any more penguins on to the finger of land.

I camped again that night in the wilds of

Punta Tombo, at some small distance from the penguins, and some of the inquisitive birds came and watched me as I worked. Although they soon lost interest, they were quickly replaced by others as I pitched the tent and made my dinner of potatoes boiled in seawater, which I ate with butter and tinned fish.

In the morning they watched me eat breakfast, strike camp and set off again. Having reached the southern extremity of my journey by travelling as close to the Atlantic Ocean as possible, I headed north once more, hugging the western side of the country.

On this particular day I stopped shortly before sunset with the foothills of the Cordillera, the mighty Andes, just visible. I rode the bike about 500 yards away from the road and set up my tent between the tufts of pampas grass, which grows at an extraordinary rate to reach heights of six feet and more. I was well out of sight of the road and there was no likelihood of anyone finding me by chance.

I had a small, robust canvas tent, with a very modern feature, an integral groundsheet. There were no zips but the flaps tied with laces.

I prepared my food over my little alcohol stove, wrote up my travel log, completed my check of the bike and its tyres, and retired to bed. The weather was cool and I was snug inside my sleeping bag. The waning moon had not yet risen and so the evening was lit only by the stars. Otherwise, everything was perfectly dark. I was tired and soon fell fast asleep.

Suddenly, I was wide awake. The moon, in its

last quarter, had risen while I slept and was now above the horizon.

Why had I woken with such a start? I listened. I could hear footsteps — slow, stealthy, deliberate footsteps — no mistake . . . very quiet . . . approaching the tent — and more than one set!

I was straining with every fibre of my being to hear clues as to who was approaching. My heart was beating fast and I kept my breathing quick and shallow to reduce the sound.

There were other night noises, too. Gentle zephyrs stirred the pampas grass and insects scurried. But there it was again, footfalls on the soft dry earth. I felt them as much as heard them. It was quite distinct, unmistakeable.

Who could be creeping up on me and why? If their intentions had been honourable, surely they would have called out from a long distance and declared themselves, not come creeping up like a thief in the night?

The noises were off to my right-hand side, of that I was certain. I unzipped my sleeping bag soundlessly. I could feel each tooth of the zip release as I eased it down until I could slip my legs out. I was wearing a T-shirt and shorts. My mind was racing. Two adversaries at least! What weapons did I have? All I had was a *facón*, a stout gaucho knife, and that was it. What use would that be? If they were armed and intent on theft they could shoot me, take what they wanted and no one would ever discover my bones. In all probability, mine were the first human feet to touch that particular piece of earth, such was the remoteness of the province of Chubut and

170

the landscape where I found myself.

The footfalls were getting closer now. They were plainly audible, as though persons unknown were creeping as stealthily as a fox on the dry turf.

I was going to be fighting for my life at any moment. Surprise was my only chance. I must not be trapped inside the tent or I'd be helpless. If I hadn't been so stupid, if only I'd bought a gun, I wouldn't be in this mess now! I should never have been so reckless as to travel alone. I cursed my yearning for adventure. The footsteps were within a few yards now and all I had was one lousy knife and a feeble torch.

I planned my moves as I slipped the knots tying the flaps of the tent. I'd spring from the tent with the torch and knife and shout 'bang' as loudly as I could. The surprise might possibly give me the advantage for just long enough to get in the first strike.

I was ready, and the footfalls were now at the head of the tent. I could hear breathing. Five yards, less! It was now or never!

I sprang from the tent with the torch switched on, screaming, 'Bang! Bang! Bang!' as though my life depended on it, which of course it did. My knife flashed in the torchlight as I made a frenzied charge at my assailants. Euan, my Buenos Aires drinking companion, would have been proud of me.

I was promptly dazzled by two huge blinding white lights, which blazed back at me from the darkness. It took just a second for me to comprehend that my torchlight was being reflected by the eyes of a terrified, wandering cow that found itself being rudely attacked in the middle of the night by a wholly demented Englishman, who was evidently intent on slaughter or worse. With a frenzied bellow of panic, the cow turned tail and fled. Its footsteps, which again I felt as much as heard, receded rapidly into the darkness.

Shaking with fear, laughter and the early-morning chill, I followed the retreating miscreant bovine with the beam of the torch until I could see and hear her no more. I turned off the light and looked at the old crescent moon, now giving some form to the clumps of pampas grass below. Orion, the celestial hunter, was high in the sky of the southern hemisphere. He was towering above me proudly with his sword held erect and ready to fight, as I stood there on the ground, mirroring his stance.

'Who needs a gun when we have our swords?' he seemed to be asking. Obviously, he didn't have the slightest clue just how frightened I had been or how certain that I was in mortal danger. Feeling very foolish, I went back to my sleeping bag, resolving never to tell anyone just how close that cow had come to meeting its maker — had I been carrying a gun.

On the morrow I set off once more for the long ride back to Bahía Blanca. Main roads in the more remote parts of Argentina are straight as arrows for miles on end and hours sometimes elapsed between seeing other road users. The weather was fine and unhurried ranks of white fluffy clouds stretched away to the distant horizon. I enjoyed the flat, unvarying landscape of the pampas gliding smoothly by as I pondered Juan Salvado's future. I was pleased the trip had demonstrated that, with my resources alone, it was possible for me to take the penguin to find his kin, if I could improvise some method of carrying him all that distance, but I was saddened by the thought of his departure. It certainly wouldn't be an easy trip for the penguin, and I'd have to be certain that the hardships and privations of such a journey were the best option.

I was still an hour's ride away from Bahía Blanca when I felt a sudden lurch and the bike's engine petered out. Different emotions surged through me — principally frustration and hopelessness — as I considered pushing the bike for miles. At moments like this, the bike was becoming a Sisyphean punishment. I disengaged the clutch and allowed the bike to freewheel along as far as possible as I analysed the last sounds I had heard from the engine. There had been no spluttering, just a sudden cut-out, so electrics were a more likely cause than a fuel problem, but had there been an expensive-sounding *clink* just before? I checked the spark plug and fuel line and felt increasingly concerned when I found that neither of these usual, easily rectifiable problems were the cause of the stoppage. Within a short time I had discovered the broken exhaust valve rocker arm, which I couldn't possibly repair at the roadside. With a sense of despair I started pushing the machine along the flat road.

I had been going for no more than twenty minutes when, to my delight and immense relief, a car drove past and stopped. After the driver had controlled his mirth at the thought of my relying on the motorbike for such a mission, he offered to tow me to the town. He promised he'd drive slowly. Holding two turns of the rope around the handlebars, which I could release quickly in the event of an emergency, we set off at a terrifying, breakneck speed. Only the thought of pushing the bike for thirty miles prevented me from abandoning my rescuer. On reaching Bahía Blanca, however, he drove sensibly, to my surprise, and even took me to the station, where I was able to catch the train as planned. I counted myself lucky. If the breakdown had happened in a really remote place I might have had to wait days for assistance or been forced to abandon the bike altogether.

During the long train journey back to Buenos Aires I made the decision to give up any attempt to reunite Juan Salvado with wild penguins. This latest breakdown made all thoughts of trusting the unreliable bike absurd. Of all the options that I had put together in the Harrods tea room, the most satisfactory appeared to be keeping him at St George's. Juan Salvado certainly wasn't unhappy living there and, in truth, I hated the thought of parting company with him. I'd had enough of crossing bridges before I'd got to them.

I would carry on as before and trust Juan Salvado to tell me what was best for him. 'Sufficient until the day is the evil thereof!' This would be our motto.

174

15

The Quest for El Dorado

In which I find what I went looking for

I had gone to South America for the principal purpose of meeting people, exploring places and seeing wildlife far from my knowledge and experience. Having grown up in the gentle, fertile rolling fields and wooded downs of Sussex, I yearned to experience the thin-air heights of the mighty Andes, the vast empty plains of Patagonia, the snowy pine-covered wilderness of Tierra del Fuego and the arid, drifting desert sands of the Atacama. I longed to see the enormous waterfalls of Iguasú, the volcano of El Misti and witness the Inca civilization of Cuzco and Machu Picchu. I sought the magic of Lake Titicaca and to hear the thunder of the remarkable glacier of Perito Moreno. To meet and understand the peoples of those places and to explore all the lands in between was what I most desired; I wanted to learn from the inhabitants, whose language and customs were completely alien to me, and to have the opportunity to observe for myself some of the flora and fauna of that continent.

I craved the freedom to escape from the safe, ordered security of gentle, rural England and to take real responsibility for the choices I made. I wanted to find my 'road less traveled by' and to see where it led. I wanted to experience some of life's challenges without the security of a safety net. If there are always cows in the field, hens in the barn and dinner on the table, where is the challenge and excitement? I wanted to travel steerage and rough it for a while; to find out what Fate would drop into my life, if only it had the opportunity.

The reality, of course, was often vastly different from my expectations and there were moments when my resolve was sorely tested.

On my first expedition to the south of Bolivia in the high Andes, while Juan Salvado was lodging with friends, I was making my way to Potosí, a town renowned for its silver mines, from where I intended to fly back to Argentina. I had spent the night in a rudimentary hostel in a one-horse town not far from my destination. After checking out in the morning, I took almost all of the remaining notes out of my money belt, put them in my pocket and made my way to an agency to buy tickets for my bus journey and flight. By chance, a carnival procession was taking place and I stopped en route to watch. There was a great crush of people in the plaza as the crowd jostled for the best view and there was much noise and pageantry from the parade. The brilliance of colour and light at that altitude, like the sound of the pipes and drums, is unforgettable. Even my drab old blue duffel coat seemed to take on the lustre of a peacock's plumage.

After a short while I turned to leave but, on checking my pockets, I found to my horror that I had been robbed. I knew there was no point in shouting 'Stop! Thief!' in either English or in Spanish since practically no one in the crowd spoke the former and very few the latter. An artful little pickpocket had struck and then melted away. What would have been the point in alerting the local police? The crook was undoubtedly long gone. Very swiftly, I came to the conclusion there was nothing to be done but learn another lesson the hard way.

In total I had lost about US$60 which, of course, had far more buying power in those days. I had nothing left besides some loose change and the clothes I stood up in. I could possibly have obtained funds by finding a bank and then attempting to grapple with the communication systems between the pueblo and London or Buenos Aires. I could probably have returned to my cheap hotel and tried to get help there. Instead, I decided to rely on my own resources to get as far as the border, where I would be able to access my Argentine bank account. This resulted in some very long periods of walking punctuated by occasional rides in rickety old trucks and dilapidated shooting brakes that were trundling past — I was extremely grateful to the owners for their assistance.

Late in the afternoon on the first day I arrived in a tiny little hamlet of about six houses. This unremarkable oasis with its little spring and sparse greenery was a few miles off my planned route but I had been assured by the driver who had given me a lift that there was a good possibility I might find a bed for the night. Sure enough, in return for a few coins I was given food and shelter by a family who lived in a very simply constructed peasant shack.

There were seven in the family: a mother and her six children, three in their teens and three younger, although I was told later that night there had been others who had died. The father, too, had died a couple of years before. No reason was offered and I thought better of asking.

Their clothes were a mixture of homespun and cast-offs. The younger ones didn't have shoes and those of their elders were so damaged and beyond any useful life that I almost wondered why they bothered wearing them at all unless it was a question of pride. Their house was made of sun-baked mud bricks under a roof of tiles made the same way. It comprised four small rooms, having grown room by room along with the family's requirements, as a result of which none of the floors or lean-to roofs lined up. Cooking was done over an open fire in a large metal pot, which was added to each day, and that evening we ate a stew made up of goat and maize, beans and polenta. When the sun went down we huddled into one of the rooms, where we sat together on skins and blankets. Some of the neighbours came in, too, out of curiosity. There we struggled, with good humour, to understand each other.

I learned that infant mortality was high. I discovered that, although they could count, my new friends were essentially illiterate. They lived by keeping many goats, a few hens and growing what crops they could. At night the livestock was penned by the house to protect it from pumas, large wild cats that could easily take a goat (and a small child, I warranted).

They showed me the crude loom they used for making the blankets, which I found intriguing and wanted to see working. The little children were greatly amused that I was able to read but didn't know how to weave; obviously my priorities were badly mixed up! The men smoked pipes, chewed coca leaves and drank locally made cane spirit at a rate that was only a little faster than the women. Thus the evening wore on. The children nestled up close together and fell asleep, as did the adults, later, once the alcohol took hold. We all snuggled close under skins and blankets against the extreme cold of the high Altiplano night. It was definitely a new experience for me to be huddled up with so many complete strangers. Their generosity moved me — a young man in his selfish twenties — for while they had so little, they shared what they had with a traveller that night.

In the morning the women were up first, lighting the fires and baking bread for breakfast. The men got going more slowly and appeared to be considerably more hungover. I was delighted when they offered to show me around the village after breakfast. It was impossible not to admire the sturdy goat pens, the neat rows of crops, the hand-woven fabrics and the nobility of spirit displayed by the villagers as they talked about their lives with pride. Although the most desirable parts of the continent had been seized by the Europeans in the names of their deities and rulers, leaving those members of the indigenous population who survived the violence and the

179

foreign diseases with only the most inhospitable regions, their descendants still clung on to a traditional way of life with fierce independence. So it was with real sorrow that they explained how all their lives were changing as the younger generations insisted upon looking for work in the towns, rather than staying to support the villages that raised them.

Feeling the experience had left me both humbled and enriched, and had more than compensated for my pecuniary loss, I continued my journey.

By day the very thin air of the high Andes offers little protection from the searing sun and by night the starlight is equally unimpeded. Those mountain ranges provide better views of the night sky than anywhere else on earth, which is why so many international observatories are situated there. The firmament, I discovered, is the most perfect inky-blackness from which the Milky Way blazes, as though Apollo's hand had sloshed white paint right across the heavens with a brush. The stars of familiar constellations become lost against the hundred thousand million stars of our galaxy, all of which appear to be visible. I was amazed to discover that to the naked eye there are no really dark parts of the Milky Way at all. Away from the main disc of the galaxy, other stars shine out fiercely from the darkness, steady and brilliant. Even without a moon there is sufficient light to navigate on foot along the roads and paths without difficulty. But without the thick blanketing atmosphere, which at lower altitudes obscures most of the brilliance and beauty of the cosmos, the bitter cold can be unendurable.

On the second night, I didn't look for shelter. I'm embarrassed to admit it now, but the smell of the unwashed people, clothing, blankets and badly cured skins of the night before had been extremely pungent. I expect my hosts felt exactly the same about me. Consequently, I thought a night in the open couldn't be worse, so I decided to walk on through the star-lit night aided by the light of a waning moon which rose an hour or two before dawn. But during the darkness I became cold, very cold; I became so extremely cold that I began to understand how people can freeze to death. Try as I might, I couldn't keep warm. Running or jogging isn't an option; the air is too thin and exhaustion sets in very quickly. With insufficient air to exercise, yet in temperatures far too cold not to, the ill-equipped traveller finds himself in a perilous situation. By the time the sky eventually lightened in the east, I was so cold I could scarcely force one leg in front of the other. I stood still as the upper limb of the sun eventually broke the horizon and I felt, almost instantly, the reviving warmth on my face. As the sun rose, I luxuriated in its bounty, like a lizard on a stone. I had made it.

It was not a good experience and not one I would willingly repeat without adequate protection, notwithstanding the awe-inspiring majesty of the universe as few see it. In hindsight, the night in the rustic hut had been hugely preferable. I had never deliberately courted danger and that night spent in the open so high up was an imprudent decision, I will concede now, but I did enjoy the experience of self-reliance over the course of those years and have carried memories of those adventures ever since.

Still, for all the occasions when things didn't quite go according to my plans there were others when I couldn't have devised any improvement in the unrolling of events. After all, the timing of my stay in Punta del Este was pivotal for my fateful encounter with Juan Salvado. The coincidence happened as I was making my way home following a remarkable three-week stay in Paraguay, courtesy of an invitation from the Williams family, whose son Danny was in his final year at St George's.

Alfred Williams, Danny's father, had timed a business meeting in Buenos Aires to coincide with the end of term and had then flown all of us back to Paraguay in his plane. Thanks to the pilot's skilful low-level flying, I was given an opportunity to see how, during the passage of millennia, the course of the Paraguay River had meandered for dozens of miles either side of its current location, creating vast impenetrable wetlands and countless thousands of ox-bow lakes, which glinted in the sunlight as we passed. Those flatlands are a haven for wildlife. From this privileged perspective, I saw great clouds of birds take to the air from dense jungle and family groups of capybara — an enormous rodent which grows to the size of a large pig — flee as we disturbed them in their watery home. I found it hard to believe my luck.

After a few days at the Williams's grand house in Asunción, the Paraguayan capital, Alfred, Danny, a school friend of Danny's named Jack and I flew to the extreme south-east of the country to live the life of gauchos for a couple of weeks in the 'camp' (an Anglicization of *campo*, meaning farmed land). Chongo, the pilot, located the cattle — a herd of thousands — by flying systematically over the estancia, before we returned to land on a grass strip alongside the hacienda.

We collected such provisions as we required — maize, fruit and essentials to supplement the workers' rations along with some chocolate, an unaccustomed luxury for them. Within a couple of hours we had saddled up the tough little ponies and set off to find the herd. Progress was not quick in those wild lands, which are a mixture of grassland and scrub, riddled with armadillo holes. It wasn't until the late morning of the second day that we encountered the cattle again.

Living among the gauchos who worked on the Williams's cattle ranch was a superb experience. The estancia was not like an English farm. It had no fences and was instead more savannah-like, with poor grass and shrubby trees which grew to some thirty feet. Where an English farm is measured in hundreds of acres, South American estancias can occupy hundreds of square miles — about 150 in the Williams's case. It was just a little bigger than the Isle of Wight.

The gauchos lived with the cattle and drove them on to pastures new each day. The land was poor and the search for fresh grass unrelenting. The men lived in the saddle and collected new supplies from the hacienda only every few weeks. Their horsemanship was superb, as would be expected of anyone who has lived in the saddle from childhood. The life of a gaucho was a seamless combination of working, eating, sleeping and entertainment, and it was often impossible to determine which of those things was being done at any given time.

At sunset a camp would be made, fires lit, food prepared, songs sung and sleep taken under the stars. The life of these gauchos and peons (the former are skilled cowboys while the latter are semi-skilled workers) was very simple and extremely hard. The epic poem of Martín Fierro, written in the 1870s, described something of their life which hadn't noticeably changed a century later.

> *My glory is living freely as the birds of the air;*
> *I make no earthly nest where there is much suffering,*
> *And nobody can follow when I again take flight.*
> *I have no lover to vex me with quarrels;*
> *Like the beautiful birds that hop between branches,*
> *I make my bed of clover and stars are my covers.*

All of a gaucho's possessions had to be carried with him on his horse. A saddle, a bedroll, a folding tripod stool, a *facón* (which, with a blade up to a foot long, was often worn on the back), a few coins and decorative silverware, a gun and lasso, together with a small hollowed gourd, decorated with silver, from which they would drink *mate* at every opportunity through a metal straw. That was about the sum of it.

If they became ill they either survived with the skills and herb lore of their fellows or they died and were buried where they fell. Not for them the support of emergency services.

These men were of Guarani Indian blood and spoke little Spanish that I could understand. They were small, dark, wizened, sinewy, tooth-challenged and leathery and as hard as the baked earth from which they wrested their living. They appeared to smile all the time, although at first I found that discomfiting, because the smiles looked more like maniacal grins.

The estancia was bordered to the east by the Paraná River. There were no roads on the estancia and no metalled road led to it. These were truly wild lands. If a crime was committed, these men were judge and jury. There was no form of authority or law to protect them from the criminals and outlaws who roamed the borderlands pretty much at will, and who lived by taking what they wanted wherever they could find it . . . if they could get away with it. The gauchos didn't expect outside interference and certainly wouldn't have thanked anyone for trying to provide it either; these were men who were used to looking after themselves. Cattle rustlers from over the border, whom they called *brasileños*, were troublesome at times but, I was told, not many of the *brasileños* ever had a second chance to try to steal from Don Alfredo.

The gauchos' staple diet was meat. On one occasion while I was there, several armadillos were caught and, in the evening, they were gutted, thickly wrapped in mud from the riverbank and rolled into the embers of a fire. An hour or so later the baked mud balls were broken open to reveal the pale, juicy, steaming and succulent flesh from which the bones and shell simply fell away. A seven-banded armadillo grows to about thirty inches in length and has as much meat as a very large chicken. It tastes more like strong pork than anything else. Eaten with a light sprinkling of charcoal, the mud of the cooking case and the dust of a Paraguayan cattle drive, from a tin plate, using fingers and a stone-sharpened *facón*, wearing a peon's *bombachas* and poncho, sitting on the warm sun-baked earth and leaning against a sheep's pelt saddle roll, the air filled with a thousand new smells, listening to Guarani songs as the moon rose and the campfire died down: such were the ingredients for just about the most memorable meal of my life. Quite simply, each one of my senses — feeling, hearing, sight, taste and smell — was buzzing and tingling with the electricity of totally new sensations. This indeed was what I had come to South America for. In that brief and shining moment, I had found my El Dorado.

I fell asleep under the stars that night

dreaming of giving it all up and living the life of a gaucho. It would have been far too gruelling and probably too limiting after a while but, at that moment, it was simply a glorious romance to be able to play cowboys for real.

Each night I slept like a log until first light, when I would be kicked into life by Danny, who took the greatest delight in the reversal of authority away from college. Each day, with his help, I learned new skills. He was only five years younger than me and had spent a great deal of time with the gauchos, perfecting their way of riding over years in their company. The peons' riding style was quite different from the English school I had learned as a child. One wouldn't describe it as kind. Hell-for-leather, hard-mouthed, devil-may-care was the nature of it and, until I accepted that, neither the ponies nor the peons were co-operative. After a very short time, I admitted I had to learn to ride as they did, for my pony gave me no choice; he simply didn't respond to being handled the English way. However, once I had that sorted — or, should I say, once he had that sorted — we got on tolerably well.

Although direct communication between these men and me was very limited, they showed me how to do the things their lives required. I'd like to think it was because I tried to copy their words and their ways that I was accepted, especially by the younger men. I tried to look at life through their eyes and not my own; I attempted to acquire their skills and to laugh at the things they laughed at (which was mainly me!). So I was able to observe a way of life that had gone unchanged for a couple of centuries, but which was, at that moment, on the point of being lost for ever.

A gaucho's superb skill with the lasso has to be seen to be truly appreciated but I'll try to create a picture. We arrived at one encampment with a shortage in our meat supplies. A few of the men mounted up and, with me in their wake, set off in search of a cow to supplement our rations. They made their selection by frightening a number of cattle into stampeding, then skilfully kept them running in circles of a few hundred yards until they had identified their victim. I should add here that while a gaucho could easily ride his pony bareback he would never be without his saddle, which was a crucial part of his equipment, needed not only to carry his few possessions but also as a working tool in its own right.

Target selected, one of the riders then started working his lasso. The gaucho lasso is made of supple braided pony leather and terminates in a heavy four-inch metal ring, through which the leather rope runs freely. The weight of the ring helps give momentum to the lasso when its gyrating loop is being wielded, single-handed, above the head. At the same time, in his other hand, the gaucho holds the reins and controls his galloping steed.

The gaucho's pony can outrun the cows, which allows the rider to throw the spinning loop of the lasso over the steer's head, where it drops round the animal's neck or horns. As it falls, the gaucho winds his end of the lasso round the pommel of his saddle. Skilfully, he now slows down and works the panicked cow towards a tree. Then, using the tree as a pulley block, he slowly draws the cow on until its horns are locked against the trunk. The cow strains with all its might, not against the lasso or the gaucho, but against the tree; therein lies the skill. At the crucial moment, one of the peons, holding his reins and pommel in one hand and his *facón* in the other, canters past the cow and, in one fluid action, he slides from the saddle, feet together, merely brushing the ground, and slits the throat of the immobilized cow. He springs lightly back into his saddle and is away before the blood gushes out — it can spurt thirty feet or more. The gaucho releases the tension from the lasso and dismounts. The cow bellows, its eyes roll and slowly it sinks to its knees as its life pumps out. Before it falls, the proud gaucho must walk up to within inches of the horns of the dying animal and remove the lasso.

On this occasion, as on every occasion, I imagined, there was much shouting, cheering and gesticulation among the other gauchos and peons as they congratulated the few whose skills had provided them with entertainment and food. Before long, fresh meat was being roasted over red-hot embers freshly raked away from a roaring fire.

After the slaughter of a cow, such meat as the peons could carry with them would be divided up, the rest of the body abandoned. I once saw the major parts of a carcass rolled into the river and then watched as flashes of silver began to flicker around it. Crescendo is a good simile.

189

Within a few short moments, tranquil river water exploded into a seething, boiling eruption of frenzied red and silver-gold. Minutes later, the piranhas had all departed and bare bones lay in waters that were still once more. That grizzly spectacle certainly deterred me from indiscriminate swimming in the river at the end of a day's ride.

It was with a heavy heart I left that beautiful and intriguing country. Little did I appreciate, however, the timing had been ordained by destiny so that I should be in Punta del Este at precisely the same moment as a certain penguin.

Whether travelling by train or truck, bus or bike, horse or Shanks's pony, I discovered moments of profound fulfilment and contentment in South America. With Juan Salvado safely staying with friends, I set out for the southern extremity, Tierra del Fuego, and from there I crossed into southern Chile. I spent a full week without seeing another living soul, apart from penguins, and totally out of communication. By day I walked amid the snow-capped mountains, and in deep valleys, where the ground was so covered with waist-high daisies that they appeared, from a distance, to be as white as the towering peaks. By night I camped in the great forests of southern beech trees and cooked my meagre rations on a wood fire. All I carried was some fruit and a little flour, sugar and butter, from which I made crude pancakes. It was Elysian.

190

Travelling alone gave me ample opportunity to reflect on all that I had seen and heard, to compare the reality of South America to my preconceptions and to consider what was truly important and of real value. How, in a world so full of astonishing beauty and priceless wonders, had humans devised so much misery, and not just for our own species? The essence of being human and the nature of friendship were recurring issues of my contemplations. However interesting or entertaining they may have been, such *compañeros* as I met along life's byways who shared a journey, a campfire, a cooking pot or even a tent for a while, were simply ships that passed in the night. I would never have opened my heart to them as I had to Juan Salvado and the same was true of all those who encountered him. How was it that a penguin brought such comfort and tranquillity to the people whose lives he touched? Why did they go to his terrace and bare their souls to him as though they had known him for a lifetime, treating him like a real friend who could be relied upon in adversity? Was it peculiar to those times of violence and despair and would it have been different in periods of peace and prosperity?

It certainly appeared that people confided more willingly in Juan Salvado than in their fellows. Such, it seems, is simply the nature of humans with penguins.

'How was it that a penguin brought such comfort and tranquillity to the people whose lives he touched?'

16

Can I Swim?

In which Juan Salvador at last returns to the water

From the very first day that I brought a penguin to live at St George's, one youngster in particular wanted to help with the care of Juan Salvado and his name was Diego Gonzales. Diego found life difficult, more so than most. He was a Bolivian boy; his father was of European descent and his mother indigenous Bolivian. The offspring of such unions were traditionally called *mestizo* in Latin America, a term which was considered descriptive and not insulting necessarily, but nevertheless he was occasionally the butt of unkind comments from the other boys.

Diego arrived at School House a diffident, shy thirteen-year-old lad, who gave the impression of being frightened by his own shadow. He was not an academically gifted boy and he really struggled with his work. In the competitive atmosphere of the college, his shortcomings were always apparent. Fortnightly orders, where students were placed in rank order of their academic results, were intended to be an incentive to work hard and improve, but they certainly didn't help Diego.

Sadly, none of the many and varied extra-curricular activities seemed to suit Diego either.

He was a slightly built boy whose motor skills and coordination appeared to be well below average for his age; he couldn't catch a ball to save his life. On a rugby field, he was gaunt, cold and miserable, even on the warmest of days. His oversized games shirt hung limply on his narrow frame, almost hiding his shorts from which his spindly legs protruded, and his sleeves hung down so low that only his fingertips were visible. Nobody passed the ball to him or involved him in the game, except to plague him. If the ball came his way, it usually struck him heavily on the chest as though it had taken him by surprise and he invariably fumbled the pass.

Diego's early education had not equipped him well for life in the college. His knowledge of English was decidedly limited and even his Spanish was heavily laced with the patois of the Bolivian *mestizos*, so he was a taciturn boy who avoided conversation. He hadn't been taught to look after his possessions nor how to organize them. It was generally beyond him to have the right things for lessons or kit for games. But, for me, the saddest part of all was the home-sickness from which he suffered. He hadn't been ready to leave home and he missed it dreadfully. In almost every way, Diego was young for his age.

The college, like all communities, had many good qualities. There was a well-structured pastoral system and each new boy was assigned an older boy who was responsible for looking after his younger charge for the first two or three weeks. In turn, these 'old lags' were supervised by a prefectorial system, which was overseen by responsible residential staff who were well aware of Diego's difficulties. It must be remembered that the overwhelming majority of the boys who went through the college flourished. They enjoyed their lives there and made strong and lasting friendships. Diego was just the worst case of a fish out of water.

It came as no surprise, therefore, that Diego really enjoyed the company of Juan Salvado and spent as much time with him as he could. While on the roof terrace he was out of sight of most of the college and he could relax. Diego was not without friends, but they were boys like him who had similar problems adapting to the ethos of the school. The boys who did not enjoy a daily surfeit of rugby were sometimes considered to be 'weaker brethren'.

The responsibility for looking after Juan Salvado was good for those boys. They were un-failingly dutiful in getting supplies of sprats from the market, in maintaining the cleanliness of the terrace and in keeping Juan Salvado company. Even more pleasing was how much genuine fun they seemed to have in the process. Daily life must have been ridden with anxieties for the unhappi-est among them and it was a relief to see them enjoying the penguin, free for a while from the constraints of classrooms, social hierarchies and worries about their families far away.

The education offered at St George's had more novel features than just a penguin living on the terrace of one of the assistant masters. The swimming pool, for example, was unusual because it was completely devoid of any filtration plant or chlorination system at all. This deficiency was compensated for by emptying the pool completely once every fortnight, by which time the water would be a fairly opaque green and often had a large colony of toads living in its depths. Today's readers might be daunted by this thought but, at that time, all the pupils would have bathed habitually and without adverse effects in the warmish, languid, silt-laden, swampy-banked rivers, teeming with abundant wildlife, that meandered across their homeland. Nowadays many would mistakenly believe such waterways to be 'polluted' simply because they were toffee-brown in colour. Be that as it may, the less than pellucid pool at St George's hardly merited comment at the time.

Once the temperature in Buenos Aires began to rise, the college swimming pool was drained of its stagnant winter contents, scrubbed clean and filled afresh with water pumped from our own wells fed from aquifers deep underground. Once commissioned, the cleaning cycle of the pool continued — every two weeks — until the end of the season.

The possibility of letting Juan Salvado free in the pool had occurred to me, of course, but when he first came to live at the college during the winter months, the water was foul. I reasoned that by the time his feathers had become waterproof again, the swimming pool would be in operation.

The majority of the boys were generally enthusiastic about swimming but, like tennis and *paleta* (an Argentine version of squash, played in an open-air court), it wasn't a major sport — mainly because it wasn't rugby. However, it was greatly enjoyed as a recreation on summer evenings after prep, when the water was clean and the weather warm.

It hadn't been a notably warm start to the season that year, so by the end of the pool's first fortnight in operation, the water wasn't particularly inviting, but neither was it particularly green; indeed, the lane markers painted on the bottom were still plainly visible. Only a small number of intrepid boys wanted to swim after prep that evening and after twenty minutes even the hardiest had exited the water and gone back to their houses for a hot shower.

As soon as the swimmers had departed, I signalled Diego and two of his friends, who were exercising Juan Salvado on the playing fields nearby, to bring him to the enclosure so that we could see if he would swim.

I had purposefully waited for this specific evening, the one scheduled for the routine maintenance of the swimming pool, so that I could address the remaining reservations I had about letting Juan Salvado use it. No one would object if he fouled the water just before it was drained and, if he refused to get out when I wanted him to, I would certainly be able to retrieve him once the pool was emptied.

Juan Salvado had been living at the college for several months by then and, in all that time, he had never been able to swim freely. His grey-stained tummy feathers had become steadily whiter and now he looked fit and normal, for a penguin, and I judged that this was the window of opportunity I had been waiting for.

Although he knew much of the college grounds, Juan Salvado hadn't yet visited the pool enclosure. Diego placed him next to me and, as I walked to the water's edge, Juan Salvado followed in my footsteps. He surveyed the still water in the pool without apparently comprehending its nature.

'*Go on!*' I said, miming a dive into the pool and gesticulating with a swimming action. He looked at me, then at the water. '*It's all right, you can swim!*' I said, bending down and splashing a little water on him.

Juan Salvado looked me straight in the eyes and asked, '*Ah! Is this where the fish come from?*' Then, without further encouragement, he launched himself from the edge. With a single flip of his wings, he flew like an arrow from a bow straight across the pool and collided headlong with the wall on the opposite side, face first, while travelling at considerable speed. The impact was palpable. There was a groan and a sharp intake of breath from the watching boys. Juan Salvado rose to the surface spluttering and dazed. He paddled about giving little jerks of his head. I thought he might have broken his neck but, after a moment, he gave a vigorous shake in characteristic penguin-fashion and ducked below the surface again.

I had never before had the opportunity to

study a penguin in the water at such close range. I had become thoroughly familiar with Juan Salvado's clumsy and amusing bipedal progress on land, but now I watched in awe. With his legs and feet trailing astern, he swam with his wings. Using only a stroke or two, he flew at great speed from one end of the pool to the other, executing dramatic turns before touching the sides. It was a bravura performance of aquatic acrobatics, a master class, as he passed within a hair's breadth of the sides of the pool without so much as brushing against them, let alone suffering another impact. Using the full volume of the twenty-five-metre swimming pool, he looped the loop and leaped out of the water. Then, falling back, he dived to the bottom and raced from one end to the other before turning on a sixpence and corkscrewing back. The only comparison that could be drawn with this exhibition of total mastery of three-dimensional space would be a bird in flight, although the speed of an expert ice skater on a rink is a good comparison for such skill in spatial awareness. It was clear to me now how badly he needed to use those great wing muscles that had been idle too long. Juan Salvado had finally found some freedom to express his true nature, his independence, and to show us all just what it meant to be a penguin.

Possibly the joy of flying described by Jonathan Livingston Seagull in his story is the nearest one can get to the obvious exuberance Juan Salvado displayed that evening. All the watchers were spellbound. A gymnast's floor exercise, by comparison with Juan Salvado's exhibition, would have seemed leaden and two-dimensional.

The sheer enjoyment that the penguin appeared to derive from his superlative control in the water communicated itself to the spectators. Juan Salvado could fly through the water many times faster than the swiftest Olympic swimmer — a length took him a couple of seconds, a distance that would take a human about fifteen. Juan Salvado alternated his sub-aquatic demonstrations with intervals swimming on the surface, preening himself and splashing about.

On the surface, penguins swim like neckless ducks, propelling themselves with their feet. They bob about competently, but not elegantly — hardly compelling viewing. But underwater, penguins show a consummate mastery of their element that can transfix an audience.

Diego and the other boys were as bewitched as I was. 'Look at him go!' they shouted. 'Ooooh!' and 'Ahhh!' they cooed, as though they were watching a fireworks display.

After a while Diego came over to me and asked quietly, 'Can I swim with him too?'

'What!? And it's 'May I swim',' I corrected him.

'*Sí*. May I swim? Oh, please! Five minute only.'

I was astonished! He had never gone near the pool before and I didn't even know if he could swim. Indeed, I had never known Diego actively want to do anything, apart from seek out the company of Juan Salvado and avoid the rest of the college.

'Can you swim?' I asked.

'*Sí*, what I ask you!' he said, confused. 'Oh, yes please, can I, can I swim?' he begged.

Aware of the frustration he must be having with the complexities of English, I decided the lesson could wait. The boy was actually showing an interest in something at long last.

'But the water is cold, it's going green and it's getting late now! Are you sure you want to go in?'

'Please!'

'All right then,' I said, 'but be quick!'

I had never seen him so animated before. His eyes were sparkling and he seemed to be truly alive for the first time since I had known him. He actually ran back to the house to get changed into his swimming kit and reappeared in no time. Without hesitating or pausing for final confirmation of permission, he dived into the cold, greenish water. I had more than half prepared myself to jump in and rescue him should it transpire that he couldn't swim after all, and part of me suspected he might sink to the bottom like a stone.

But, for the second time that evening, I was astonished. Not only could Diego swim but he swam magnificently! He chased after Juan Salvado and, whereas with anyone else it would have looked absurd, Diego swam so elegantly that their pairing wasn't ridiculous at all. As Diego swam, Juan Salvado swam round him, spiralling the boy. They appeared to be synchronizing their movements and swimming in unison. I had never before seen such interaction between two different species. The demonstration gave all the appearance of having been choreographed to highlight the skills of each, as in a duet written for violin and piano. Neither was principal nor subordinate.

201

Sometimes Juan Salvado took the lead and Diego swam as though chasing him. Juan Salvado allowed Diego to get close behind him and then off he would fly again. At other times Diego appeared to lead and the penguin swam round the boy, making figures of eight as though he were spinning a cocoon or weaving a spell. Occasionally they swam so close that they almost touched. This was a sublime *pas de deux* and I was entranced. Words cannot describe the magic that was in the air and the water that evening, magic that was operating on so many different levels.

I had been wondering vaguely if Juan Salvado would get out of the pool soon because it was clear that he would not come out unless of his own volition, although while Diego was swimming with him the concern remained at the back of my mind.

Diego was as good as his word. Unbidden by me, and after only a few minutes, he swam to the edge and in one graceful movement sprang out of the pool and stood with water streaming from his hair, over his shoulders and on to the floor. Next, skimming through the water, came Juan Salvado, like a homing torpedo. With a flick of his wings at the critical moment, he rocketed out of the water and came to a gliding halt, on his tummy, by my feet. We all laughed out loud.

'*There, that's how it's done. By Jove, I needed that swim! You're wrong about the fish though, I searched everywhere and couldn't find any!*'

I was almost speechless. I had witnessed an acrobatic (or should that be aquabatic?) display the likes of which I had never seen before. For technical merit and artistic interpretation it would have scored full marks from any judge, but that was not all. Standing quietly by the poolside, watching the penguin and chewing the corner of his towel, was a well-built, lithe youth who, I was confident, could outswim almost anyone in the college. It was simply a revelation. He wasn't the sad little chap we had become used to, but a very normal boy with a very special talent, and nobody in the college had realized it until that moment.

'Diego! You can swim!'

'*Sí*, I can swim, thank you.'

'No, I mean you are able to swim really well — brilliantly in fact!'

'You think?' he asked without looking directly at me but I saw just the first flicker of a smile on his face. The first, I believe, that had touched his lips since leaving Bolivia.

'Where did you learn to swim? Who taught you?'

Diego was looking at the bird. I followed his gaze and saw Juan Salvado preening his feathers with his beak as though absolutely nothing out of the ordinary had happened at all. I also observed, with huge pleasure, that he was as dry as a bone. His waterproofing was at last fully restored.

Intriguingly, the other boys only had eyes for the penguin and hadn't apparently noticed anything special about Diego. They had seen only that the penguin was a far better swimmer

203

than Diego, and were absorbed in talking about that.

As we returned to School House, Diego told me that his father had taught him to swim at their home on the river, although he had never swum competitively. He also spoke quite freely and without reserve about other things he enjoyed at home in Bolivia. It was the first time I had known him open up like this and appear willing to talk about himself, his life and his home. It was as though I were with a different boy. I listened in silence, without making any corrections to his English, as he talked non-stop all the way back to the house.

Shortly afterwards, as I was passing, I called in on Richard, the housemaster, and mentioned that I thought Diego might be 'rounding the corner'. I didn't explain further. That could wait. He was delighted to hear that I thought there were hopeful signs. 'Oh, I do hope you're right,' he said.

I went back to my rooms, picked up a glass and a bottle of wine and went out to sit on the terrace with Juan Salvado. Darkness was falling quickly, as it does in those latitudes, and the stars were coming out. The rotating stars of the Southern Cross show the passing of the seasons in the same way as the Plough does in the northern hemisphere, as it revolves about the lone Pole Star.

I always made sure I kept some sprats in reserve and I gave them, one at a time, to Juan Salvado, who ate them greedily after his evening's exertion and then settled to sleep by my feet. I sat near the parapet, looking out over the darkening fields. The cicadas were chirruping their evening song in the great eucalyptus trees, masking all other sounds. I poured some wine into the glass. It was as though I were pouring a libation in thanks to the gods that look after these things and I drank to their health.

'*I ought to write a book about you.*'

Juan Salvado looked up.

'*Why?*'

'*I think a lot of people would like to know about you,*' I said.

'*Would they? Really? What would you call it?*'

'Oh . . . er . . . What about Juan Enchanted Evening?'

Juan Salvado just shook his head, and the shudder ran all the way down to his tail as he settled back to sleep with his head on my foot. I poured a second glass of wine.

The events of that evening represented one of those extraordinary seminal moments that make teaching so worthwhile. I had witnessed something akin to an initiation ceremony, or perhaps more like a primeval rite of passage. There had been about those events a quality such that it might be described as a baptism or bar mitzvah, but actually it had been more intimate, corporal, more original and fundamental; a real change had taken place, not just an allegory. It was like an enchantment, because of the trance-like quality that left me questioning and evaluating what I had actually seen. A child had gone down to the water to swim with a penguin and, shortly after, a young man had emerged. There had been a rebirth, a new beginning. The ugly duckling had become a swan; the caterpillar had metamorphosed into a butterfly; the fish had found its way back to the water. Possibly the most astonishing part was that the boy himself hadn't yet perceived that his life was on the cusp of a radical change that night (any more than the ugly duckling knew he had become a swan). By serendipity I had seen something happen and recognized its significance, even if I couldn't explain it. Diego had done years of growing up in just a few short minutes, and Juan Salvador, the Penguin Extraordinary, had had something to do with it.

Later that evening I went to see Danny, my fellow gaucho, now Head of House. He was a cheerful, decent lad of eighteen summers who was better at rugby than at lessons but who gave his best to everything he did and was universally liked and respected. He was in his study with his deputy, Jack, the same studious and serious boy who had joined us in Paraguay, who actually thought deeply about things but said little.

I asked about our chances of winning the inter-house rugby tournament that year and Danny replied that it would be a finely balanced contest. The other houses had some very good players, and at all levels, too.

There were also house competitions in all the minor sports (i.e. every other sport apart from rugby). Their results were added to those of other house competitions to decide the annual award of the Inter-house Sports Shield.

I told Danny I thought it was about time he started to make arrangements for selecting the house swimming team. Now the pool was open there was no time to lose. I added that he should be sure to include Gonzales in the trials. He began to argue, but I said we had a responsibility to keep trying to get him involved in house activities. However, he, as Head of House, would select the team on merit alone, I promised, with no interference from me.

The pool was cleaned and refilled by the second evening and, a day later, Danny and the other prefects organized some races. I decided not to be present.

Shortly after the boys returned from the pool, a breathless Head of House and his deputy knocked on my door.

'Come in.'

'I can't believe it! Nobody can believe it,' Danny blurted out. After a short pause, he added, 'But you knew what would happen didn't you? How did you know? Why didn't you tell us?'

'Slow down, slow down! I don't have the slightest idea what you are talking about,' I lied. 'You haven't told me what you can't believe yet. From your tone I can only imagine you have won the Lottery. Do take a seat. Now, tell me what's happened, from the beginning.'

Danny and Jack pulled up chairs and Jack handed me a piece of paper with names and times recorded on it in a poolside scrawl.

I stopped teasing the boys and listened in silence while they enthused.

'Well, we asked for volunteers for swimming

heats, just as you said, and put together some races. Just one length, but that fellow Gonzales simply beat everybody hollow and in all the strokes! If it had been official timing he would even have demolished the college swimming records! I still can't believe it!'

I noted Danny had said 'that fellow Gonzales'. I couldn't have been more pleased. Rehabilitation achieved! A day earlier he would have referred to 'that drip Gonzales' or worse, but today Diego was elevated to 'that fellow'. I have said that both Danny and Jack were decent young men and I mean it. They weren't motivated by prejudice against Diego, but by the simple rule: life is what you make of it. This mantra had been instilled in them from birth by their parents, and by the college that had been chosen for their education. Until then they hadn't seen Diego make any effort to improve his own lot. The college motto was *Vestigia nulla retrorsum*, which translates loosely as 'No going back'. I knew there wouldn't be.

'It wasn't a fluke either,' said Jack, getting a word in for the first time. 'He could do it each time he tried — we timed him. He just made it look so easy!'

'And he can swim all the strokes, too,' said Danny. 'You should see his butterfly! He lifts himself almost out of the water. He can swim far better than I can,' he added generously. 'He can swim faster than anything! How did you know? Why didn't you tell us before? You did know, didn't you? That's why you wouldn't discuss it until I had a team selected on 'merit'?'

I listened until they had let it all out of their systems.

'The answer to your question, Danny, is Juan Salvado, that remarkable bird who is sleeping out on the terrace even as we speak,' I said, whereupon I related the events of the evening when Diego swam with the penguin.

There was no mistake. That was the turning point. Overnight, Diego appeared to grow three inches and was just unrecognizable in the morning. Even his clothes seemed to fit him better. He had earned the respect of his peers. Over the next few weeks he leaped up the fortnightly academic orders and became a popular member of the house. Success breeds success. When, at last, the swimming gala was held, the results were as everyone anticipated. He won every race for which he was eligible to enter and broke every college record that he was allowed to contest. The encouragements shouted by the watching boys were genuine, even from rival houses.

School House did not win the Inter-house Rugby Cup that year, missing out by a whisker. However, as a result of the points from the swimming gala, School House did win the more prestigious Inter-house Sports Shield; Diego was a hero and everyone wanted to be his friend. In time, Diego took almost every college swimming record. He even became sufficiently good at rugby to represent the college in matches and he passed all his public exams with creditable grades. And never again did he ask the question 'Can I swim?'

17

And They All Lived Happily —

In which this is no fairy story I'm afraid

Pets cannot fit into the life of the 'intrepid explorer'. They are too much of a responsibility. But Fate had made my 'path less travelled by' meet that of a penguin and I am so glad our paths crossed. I wouldn't have changed anything except for one crucial detail that has troubled me ever since. It is the gnawing canker, the cloven-hoofed incubus that has hovered over the oft-repeated history of Juan Salvador, and taunted me, as I have recounted the children's version that should have been.

I became exceptionally fond of that bird. I had gone to South America to discover the exotic, the unusual, and something about myself, and I had found all three in abundance. I enjoyed the company of Juan Salvado on our walks around the college grounds and in our talks on so many quiet evenings as the bustle of the day and the light subsided, sitting on the terrace under the stars with a glass of wine and a few late-night sprats. No one could fail to have been lifted by the welcome that bird gave me every morning and evening.

Our lives were largely dominated by routine. Juan Salvado was a fastidious bird. Every morning he would make a series of preparations for the day which involved ensuring he looked his absolute best. Every single feather received attention as the penguin placed each one precisely in order, clean and undamaged. That most dapper of little men, Hercule Poirot, was no more attentive to his appearance than Juan Salvado. Most of this operation was conducted with his beak, which worked with such delicate nimbleness. Those feathers he couldn't reach with his beak, he preened with his toes, which was something he also had a habit of doing when he had been asked a particularly challenging question, as though he were scratching his ear in concentration. And so his life in college continued, a cycle of sprats and swims, preening and pampering at the hands of his many fans.

As the holidays approached and further adventures beckoned, a colleague, Luke, volunteered to look after Juan Salvado at his house nearby. Luke was married with a little boy so from then on the penguin spent time in the holidays with them, if not with Maria, when I was away from the college. This was an excellent arrangement, enabling me to travel safe and secure in the knowledge that Juan Salvado was content and well looked after with sufficient care and company. He was happy and I was free to pursue adventures. Juan Salvado never appeared to be troubled by the summer's heat in Buenos Aires. He lived outside, where he could walk with grass underfoot, be shaded by trees and enjoy the cooling breezes from the river, splash in his tin bath and even, on occasion, swim with or without students in the school pool.

And so caring for Juan Salvado dovetailed into my college routine very easily, largely due to the enthusiastic support of the boys in term time and with Luke and Maria's assistance in the holidays. Occasionally a day dawned on which there was a particularly memorable event but most days were unremarkable; they simply flowed into one another, following the same pattern. Juan Salvado, it seemed, was a bird of routine, just as the boys in a boarding school are required to be.

That particular morning is etched in my mind. I knew what had happened before Luke said a word. I could see it in his eyes.

I had been away with friends in the south of the province, and Juan Salvado had stayed at Luke's house. I had returned late the evening before — too late to wake Luke's family and visit the bird — and after a short night's sleep had gone to collect my post first thing. That was where he found me.

'I'm so sorry,' he said. I gritted my teeth and waited, heart hammering in my chest.

'He was fine, all the time you were away, but then a couple of days ago he didn't eat anything when I went to feed him. I wasn't unduly concerned, it was hot and . . . ' His voice trailed off. 'I buried him in the garden, later the same day. I had to — it's too hot now and I didn't know when you'd be back. I couldn't wait. I am sorry.'

I nodded, grimly. The Englishman in me was cautious about betraying too much emotion, especially when I had been brought up to be as realistic as possible about the fate of animals, but inside I was crushed. 'Thanks for all you have done. I know you would have done your best,' was all I managed to say, desperately trying to keep myself together. The worst possible ending had happened. He had died unexpectedly and I hadn't been there.

I walked away to have some time for myself and to think. I made my way back to School House the long way round, following the perimeter of the rugby pitches to avoid meeting colleagues.

Wearily, I climbed the stairs and looked out of the door, over the terrace and beyond towards the river.

Whenever I approached the terrace there would be a telltale patter of feet excitedly running up and down, accompanied by the occasional squawk. These sounds had become an integral part of my college life, just as the bells that marked the changing events of the day. Now, there would be only a dreadful silence as I passed. No more would the boys knock at my door to collect fish, no more the laughter and delight that he brought to so many.

In my mind's eye I saw an egg. It was far away, on a rocky, windswept shore. Suddenly it tipped, then it cracked and a tiny chick drew its first deep breath through its beak. Emerging from the opening I saw its damp lolling head as it struggled, unsteadily, to get clear of its shell, while the parent birds watched. Next I saw the hatchling being fed. The scene changed and I

213

saw the healthy fledgling Juan Salvado following the adults down to the breaking sea which poured, hissed and foamed around the rocks and boulders, rushing up the beach, between the pebbles and stones, and then receding. He looked too young to test himself against that implacable and merciless tide. He hesitated, twice, thrice, and then he rushed after his parents into the sea and took the first strokes of his life with those remarkable wings of his, which had been honed to perfection by evolution through a million forebears. As the water closed over his head, his young muscles instinctively drove him forward through the roiling waters to break the surface again well away from the dangerous rocks. He bobbed on the surface and rolled from side to side, washing his uppermost flank with his wing. With his feet he scratched and preened his sides and head, and with his beak he tended to the feathers on his breast and back, quite untroubled by the turbulent water which constantly jostled and plucked at him.

Now I saw him again, far, far out from land, in mid-ocean, amid massive breaking waves under lowering storm clouds. In those giant seas, streaked with spume and spindrift, driven onwards by the screaming fury of a full gale, Juan Salvado, with a thousand of his kin, skimmed the surface to breathe before submerging again into the quieter waters under the waves, in pursuit of sprats. He swam, quite unperturbed by the raging storm and crashing seas. With his wings held out for balance, he surfed ahead of the steepening face of an immense ocean wave and submerged just

214

before the crest, towering above him, broke, releasing all its pent-up fury as it dashed itself to destruction. It was as though he were the spirit of the seas itself, the very essence of the ocean's life force, a distillation of all maritime mastery, and therefore quite invulnerable to the maelstrom which raged all about him. He was immune to any combination of wind and water that could possibly occur, naturally, for he was the pinnacle of Creation's art; he was in his element and he rejoiced in it.

I saw him again, back on land, standing intimately close to his mate and the first clutch of eggs he had sired, and I saw the first egg crack as he watched. I saw his expression and I recognized it. I looked and the scene changed again. Dazzling, sparkling, life-giving sunlight poured down through the warm, emerald-clear water. But then insidious wisps of oil appeared, filthy, brown, suffocating. Perfidious gossamer strands. Tentacles that kept growing, reached out to smother the sun and to burn, blind, envelop, engulf, choke and destroy those birds. Like some atrocious, ancient monster, created from the putrefaction of a different age, it had passed through the fires of Hades and had slumbered in its subterranean dungeon, but now it had been awoken and released by humans, and it was far more terrible than any hurricane; against this grotesque monstrosity the birds had no defence at all. The panicking creatures were lost, trapped, terrified and doomed; they tumbled in an incomprehensible and unspeakable death. Tides and currents eventually washed them ashore.

I saw him on the beach, in a bidet, in a bag; I saw him on a bus and in a bath. I saw him in a swimming pool and on the terrace, eating sprats with Maria. I felt his hard feathers against my fingertips as he pressed his warm body against my hand. I felt his head rest on my foot. Then he looked up at me once more before giving the inimitable penguin head shake, which ran all the way down his body to his bottom, as he settled against me in rest.

But the Spirit of the Oceans had left, my mind bubble burst, my vision misted over, as my breath caught in my throat and I whispered: '*I love you, little bird. I'll never forget you, as long as I live. Now you can join your mate and your family once more and never again be parted.*'

Should I have left him alone that day in Punta del Este? Should I have left him with his own kind and allowed Nature to finish what humans had unwittingly unleashed? Should I have left him to go travelling, in pursuit of my own adventure? What good had it done, any of it? What difference would it have made if I hadn't noticed him move, if I had just continued my walk along the beach? Was it worth feeling so wretched at this parting? It felt as though I had let him down in the end. He had crossed the Styx and the ferryman's bill was outstanding. A door had closed, denying me the opportunity of paying a debt that I needed to settle. How complicated is the tension that exists between heart and head in humans, for the emotions were entirely irrational, but I suppose it is precisely for the reconciliation of these conflicts that we hold our solemn obsequies. A need unfulfilled for me on this occasion.

I was overwhelmingly aware of the privilege it had been to have known and loved that remarkable bird. At that moment the sense of loss was almost overpowering; the pain of parting is the toll demanded by Fate for all the joy brought to us by loved ones and I felt inconsolable. He had recovered so well and appeared to be so content. What a sentimental fool I am, I thought, he was just a penguin. But what a penguin!

And so it was that I never said goodbye to Juan Salvado. '*Hasta la vista, amigo mio. Until we meet again, my friend.*' It has been something I have regretted ever since; a very private chapter that I couldn't quite close.

18

Reflections from Afar

In which I ponder Juan Salvador's legacy

Why had this penguin come to mean so much? That, at least, is easy to explain. Anybody who suddenly moves far from family and friends and the pets they love, feels a raw, vulnerable emptiness. It is inevitable, even despite the sensational compensations. Nature abhors a vacuum and it was into this space that Juan Salvado rushed. At first he occupied it and then he filled and dominated it. It wasn't big enough for him and so he stretched it, expanded it beyond measure. I didn't think about it, it just happened, and then he was gone.

Of course, time moves on and new family, friends and pets jostle for position in our hearts, but the vacancy left by previous occupants never fills. We keep our loved ones alive through our memories, our conversations and our stories but we don't necessarily choose to reveal how much they really meant. We don't have to. Anybody who has ever lost a pet knows. I haven't been any less fond of any of our dogs. Kipling warns us in his poem 'The Power of the Dog' to beware of 'giving your heart to a dog to tear'.

Our loves are not given, but only lent,
At compound interest of cent per cent.

219

Though it is not always the case, I believe,
That the longer we've kept 'em the more do
* we grieve;*
For when debts are payable, right or wrong,
A short-time loan is as bad as a long —
So why in Heaven (before we are there)
Should we give our hearts to a dog to tear?

My time with Juan Salvado, compared with the lifetime of a dog, was a 'short-term loan' but our relationship had every ounce of the same impact, if not more, because of the particular time in my life when our paths crossed. Should I have taken him from that beach against his will? An impetuous twenty-three-year-old from the English countryside, I didn't really consider the consequences of my actions beyond the immediate necessity of saving his life. I was in the happy position of being able to afford the luxury of supporting a passenger, although I sometimes wonder whether I should regard him as a passenger at all. Salvado or Salvador, saved or saviour? Both names were applicable in their way. After all, it hadn't been possible to decide who had adopted whom when he was chosen as a team mascot, or who had benefited more from the relationship he had with Diego.

As travelling companions go, Juan Salvado was demanding. He needed to be fed and watered, exercised and entertained, but by virtue of the many willing helpers at the college, the burden on me was very light. He ate some three or four kilos of sprats every week, which probably cost me a few thousand pesos a day; about as much as a couple of boxes of matches, certainly less than a bottle of beer. In return, I had something beyond price, and the responsibility at that time in my life was no doubt character forming. Like so many of the people I met on my travels in South America, Juan Salvado had so little, but gave such a lot.

His remarkable personality captivated all who met him. Not only was he a good listener, but he engaged people in conversation, answering them with his head and his eyes. There will come a time, I expect, when humans have learned enough about animal behaviour to realize that animals can communicate with us and each other to a far greater extent than we currently give them credit for and at that point this narrative will perhaps appear less fanciful. One day, I believe, we will be able to confirm that many animals have the capacity to understand and process information and experience emotions to a far more sophisticated degree than opinion currently holds.

Juan Salvado learned lessons faster than many humans I have known. The way he recognized that I intended him no harm on that first day when I was cleaning him, the way his behaviour changed so suddenly and the way he cooperated with me was nothing short of extraordinary to my way of thinking.

After that first day he showed no signs of fearing me, or any humans. In fact, he adored us. When he heard the noise and chatter of pupils moving around the college he would rush up and down the terrace in eager anticipation of company. When he heard footfalls on the stairs he would hurry across to the door, anxious to see who would come out on to his terrace. But he never stood behind the door because he instinctively understood it would have hit him.

There were many aspects of his behaviour I couldn't explain, for example, why he never went on to the rugby field when boys were playing or why he never collided with the sides of the swimming pool a second time, although he would swim within a whisker of it at great speed. I cannot explain how he appeared to know what he was allowed to do — what was safe for him to do in the realm of humans — and what was not. When walking, he never wandered off; when swimming in the pool, he would get out with the last swimmer. Perhaps the greatest mystery of his conduct, for me, was his dogged refusal to leave me and swim away after I first cleaned him.

Was Juan Salvado motivated by something more profound than an empty gut? Undoubtedly. Even when full to bursting point, he would still rush to greet new company coming to his terrace. He, too, had a need for companionship that is part of the nature of penguins. But whatever human company Juan Salvado was enjoying, the faithful bird would always come to me when I went on to the terrace. He would always choose me. It was my side to which he'd return. In so many ways our relationship was like that of dog and master, although I'm certain he wouldn't have acknowledged his role as that of the dog!

Juan Salvado was a source not only of amusement, but also of good. On seeing the bird, my colleagues would often greet us by imitating the Juan Salvado walk, bemusing the locals who were naturally far more down to earth as far as penguins were concerned. The boys told me that the ground staff called me *el loco inglés* — the mad Englishman. But there was no animosity in the nickname, just amusement and incomprehension. Undoubtedly they would never have dreamed of picking up a penguin from a beach or thought of interfering with the natural course of events. Like the gauchos on the plains and the Indians of the Andes, the lives of many of them were grindingly hard and there was no room for passengers. Some people would describe the sport that the gauchos made out of killing cows as bloodthirsty or cruel, and may question why I thought it an essential part of this story — but surely it was not as cruel as the lingering deaths and misery our 'civilized' society has exacted, and continues to wrench from individuals and whole species, through oil spills, for example? The only animals the gauchos killed, they killed for food.

Is there any chance the world's oceans can survive the damage we are causing but just don't see? In an equivalent way that millions of Marias paid indirectly for the mortgaged homes of the middle classes in Buenos Aires, thanks to inflation, it is the penguins and the rest of Nature's *descamisados* who pay the real cost of our way of life, in the only currency they have.

Since Rachel Carson published the seminal *Silent Spring* in 1962 the total number of humans has more than doubled. Simultaneously, an enormous number of species the world over, including penguins, have suffered population declines of eighty or ninety per cent and are now considered 'endangered', while others have become extinct. The hypothesis for the collapse of the human society of Easter Island by their degradation of the environment has been postulated as a model for the Malthusian global collapse of our entire species.

The way we live today illustrates human capacity for dramatic change over a very short time, yet despite knowing that our *modus vivendi* is unsustainable, our *modus operandi* has so far proved incapable of bringing about the measures necessary to allow wildlife populations even to equilibrate, let alone recover. What seems undeniable is that if the Bank of Nature's *descamisados* becomes insolvent, no amount of our money will ever bail us out.

But the abiding legacy of Juan Salvador should be one of hope and not despair. In life he brought cheer and optimism to a great many human souls at a time when there was anguish and distress, and my life has been greatly enlightened by the lessons learned from Juan Salvador — the penguin in a class of his own.

Epilogue

In which a new penguin teaches a lesson

It was the search for photographs of Juan Salvado that made me look in the old packing cases marked 'Argentina — To Sort', which had been languishing for decades at the back of the garage. Most of my pictures had been lost in a minor domestic flood years ago, but I thought it might just be possible I'd find some in there. So it was with nothing less than astonishment that I came across the rolls of cine film I had never actually watched. Never. In truth, I'd forgotten they were even there. I had sent them home from South America for processing, and my mother had stored them to await my homecoming. However, when eventually I did return, I couldn't afford a projector for them and when there was enough money for such things video had replaced cine, so there they remained, unwatched, and slowly they faded from my consciousness. It was a tantalizing moment. When exactly had I bought the cine camera? I racked my brains. Was it just possible that I had filmed the penguin?

An Internet search located the services of a very obliging retired gentleman who lives by the sea, only a short drive from our house. He opened his front door in response to my knock and revealed a veritable museum of recording equipment. Narrow paths wove between floor-to-ceiling shelves filled with every conceivable instrument ever devised for immortalizing fleeting sights and sounds. Beautiful brass contraptions mounted on polished mahogany stood cheek by jowl with crude metal cases bristling with knobs and switches. By breathing in deeply he had just enough room to navigate his empire.

'There is no kind of man-made recording I can't convert,' he boasted, 'from hieroglyphs to HD. This was made in 1896!' he said, caressing a device. Under other circumstances I could have been enthralled by his infectious enthusiasm, but today was different.

I handed over the collection of reels, each with three minutes of cine film, and agreed to come back later that day. I drove home and spent an uncomfortable afternoon with my imagination, rather like an expectant father in the days when they were excluded from childbirth.

'What are they like?' I asked him on my return, trying hard to suppress my excitement.

'You should have brought them to me years ago,' he remarked helpfully. 'They're dreadful.'

My heart fell. 'Isn't there anything on them?' I asked, fearing the worst.

'It's pretty grainy, but most of it's still there.'

My breath caught, my excitement recovered. Could Juan Salvado be there after all?

'Any penguins?' I ventured cautiously, as though fearful of frightening them away.

'Penguins? I didn't see any penguins, but there's some fantastic footage of sea lions.'

My disappointment was intense but, in truth, I

had been convinced I'd bought the cine camera long after the era of Juan Salvador the penguin.

My wife and I watched the DVD as soon as I got home and it was surprisingly moving to see the people and places of nearly forty years before: mountains, lakes and deserts, lamas, condors and sea lions, from the tropics to the tip of South America. All were captured in so much colour and detail. Forgotten names from half a world and half a lifetime away sprang without hesitation to my lips, bringing with them the inevitable flood of emotion.

But it was a bittersweet moment. The joy of finding so much on those films made the loss of my Juan Salvado photos all the more painful.

For the second time in as many days I had allowed myself to believe that my compadre might be there, hidden in these forgotten frames as though sleeping, just biding his time, awaiting his moment to burst back into my life once again. But as the DVD moved inexorably towards the end, I knew I had been cheated for ever. I was frustrated by the inconsequential moments flashing before our eyes on the television screen: a school sports day, a herd of llamas, a city square in which grinning friends raised glasses of beer and wine, wasting those valuable seconds. I couldn't even find compensation in the sea lions.

Despite the pleasure of the precious memories that we'd just watched, I would willingly have traded them all for just one single moment with Juan Salvado.

And then: 'Look!' I cried as I leaped from my chair to get closer to the screen. 'He's there! He *is* there after all! Oh, look! My dear old friend, at long last, we meet again!'

There in a swimming pool was the penguin, exactly as I remembered him. For the next glorious, wonderful, blissful two minutes and seventeen seconds, Juan Salvado and I were reunited. We watched to the end in silence; I didn't trust myself to talk. Of the penguin there was nothing more. How could I have been so remiss as to leave those films unseen for so long? I had been drawing the bird from memory for years, but now, at last, the eponymous Juan Salvador of countless Michell family bedtime stories could be seen for real; the delightful head shakes, wing flaps and bottom wiggles, which propelled him through the water in that swimming pool like an outboard motor, and which my prosaic words would never be able to capture, had been immortalized after all. Juan Salvado had been there, patiently waiting for me all the time.

Those flickering images were much better than anything I could have hoped for. They showed him in the pool fully restored to health, his brilliant white feathers gleaming in the sunshine — after a moult he showed no trace of the tar or his ordeal on the coast of Uruguay. And then there was his behaviour with the boys. After his swim he was standing at the centre of a group of about a dozen eighteen-year-olds and that charismatic bird was the focus of their attention as he preened and dried himself in the sunshine; although far shorter than they were in feet and inches, by any other measure the penguin had a stature to match them all.

Following the revelations on the DVD my first action was to capture the video clip and email it to my children, for it seemed particularly important to me that I send it to my son, living in India and almost as far from home as I had been when I'd met Juan Salvador. The second action was to look for flights to Argentina.

Within hours of deciding to make a return visit, I felt elation and the wheels of the aeroplane touching down on the runway in Buenos Aires. I was back in South America! My sojourn in this country during the 1970s had been such a large proportion of my adult life at the time, and my experiences so significant and different from everything that had preceded them, that I felt some apprehension about what Fate had in store now. On disembarking I felt again the gentle caress of the warm dry air and inhaled deeply in preparation for whatever might lie ahead. As my feet touched the ground I willed it to provide me with some new delight and fulfilment. We celebrate poets because at moments like these they say things better than the rest of us, and for me, perhaps, no one captures the essence of an adventure better than Tolkien.

The Road goes ever on and on,
Down from the door where it began,
Now far ahead the Road has gone,
And I must follow, if I can.
Pursuing it with eager feet,
Until it joins some larger way,
Where many paths and errands meet,
And whither then? I cannot say.

The trepidation I experienced as I queued at passport control was completely illogical on this occasion but it was impossible not to recall vividly the time when I had attempted to smuggle a penguin into this country, or to suppress the emotion, and I felt my heart rate increase. My first exchange with authority was with a morose officer, but he became positively affable when he noted the Argentine lilt of my rusty Spanish as we discussed the reasons for my visit and he even wished me a pleasant stay. It felt almost like coming home.

Much has changed, of course. Shoeshine boys have vanished into the mists of time. The city has been regenerating and around the docks in particular it now boasts many astonishing twenty-first-century edifices, while restored waterfront warehouses have been converted into the most desirable offices and apartments. Polluted land and waterways have been cleaned and a nature reserve now enhances that area but I was struck by a wave of nostalgia as I strolled around the well-remembered streets. Buenos Aires, always a fascinating city with its eclectic mix of architecture drawn from across classical European styles at one extreme to the gaudily painted corrugated iron houses of La Boca — the area where the poorest immigrants once lived — at the other, has lost none of its beguiling allure and vibrant energy.

Politics was in the air and with elections looming the billboards were full of posters. I was not surprised to see that the two towering iconic images of Eva Perón still dominate the immense Avenue 9th of July, the twenty-lane artery that flows through the very heart of the capital. Displayed on opposite sides of the citadel-like building that was once the Ministry of Works, the image depicting Eva at the broadcaster's microphone is connected evocatively in the viewer's mind with the radio mast that soars from the roof.

Nobody can doubt the significance of that extraordinary woman in the history of this great country. Those images seem to be more than just heritage monuments too. Posters and postcards of her are prominently on sale in the hundreds of little kiosks that stock sweets, tobacco, newspapers and periodicals all over Buenos Aires, but quite what her legacy is, however, I found very difficult to assess. Every person I asked had a different opinion.

Much to my pleasure, I discovered that Argentine wines have improved immeasurably and now stand comparison with the best. The quality of Argentine food hasn't changed at all though, and it really is as wonderful as I remember. In my view it is still possible to eat better in this country than anywhere else on earth and, interestingly, I saw very few people who were significantly over-weight, which gave me food for thought, too.

Traffic now follows the road signs and signals in an orderly fashion and pedestrians can use the crossings with assurance, but many of the trains are still old, utilitarian and quite devoid of any comfort. With tickets costing less than 2p per mile, I felt a surge of the old exhilaration that comes from setting off on a shoestring escapade anew and I yearned to do some serious travelling again and for the freedom to set out in pursuit of adventure. But my time was limited so I only explored the local old haunts, still familiar despite the decades that had elapsed. As the trains clanked and jolted, groaned and lurched along, I remembered their music fondly. After one short journey, the familiar Victorian solidity of Quilmes station hove into view and I asked myself how many times I had alighted here. Amid all the new congestion and bustle of the town, I wondered if I would be able find my way to the college, but something automatic took over and in less than twenty minutes I was standing at the gates.

My tour of St George's included some of the impressive new developments, but otherwise the school was essentially unchanged. I paused for a few moments as I looked at the terrace where once I had spent so much time and I recalled the look Juan Salvado had given me when I mentioned writing a book about him. '*Well, what took you so long?*' I could hear him asking. '*And, amigo mio . . . what took you so long to come back?*'

232

It was not a train but a superb double-decker bus (lacking any vestige of individual decoration or lucky charms) on which I found myself humming along new motorways out of Buenos Aires and towards San Clemente, a town about two hundred miles from the capital where there is a sea-life centre, and to which I had received a cordial invitation. As twilight ended and the dazzling sun broke over the horizon at the dawn of a new day, it cast shadows of infinite length across the perfect flatness of the landscape, the quintessence of La Pampa. Not for me the motor-bike of my youth on this occasion, although I cast envious and even lustful eyes over all the many machines that I saw.

In only five hours I was at the park and being shown around by Andrea, granddaughter of the founder of the centre, David Méndez.

I learned that at the same time as I found Juan Salvado in Uruguay, David Méndez, the retired owner of a seaside campsite, had come across a number of penguins on his local beach, here in Argentina, similarly devastated by oil. Like me, he had attempted to rescue some of the birds by cleaning them in his home with considerable success.

Word of David's triumph in returning penguins to the sea spread in the locality and the project grew as more damaged birds were brought in to be treated or their whereabouts reported to the indefatigable retiree. Next, his work extended to include sea lions and dolphins that had been similarly affected by oil and pollution in the local waters. Before long, people wanted to see for themselves and to support the endeavour, so in 1979, Mundo Marino was created on a newly acquired site of about one hundred acres. Today it possesses the largest sea aquarium in the southern hemisphere. Naturally, at the time I had no way of discovering David's early work in San Clemente, which was still limited to his private home, any more than David Méndez had any chance of finding out about my rescue of Juan Salvado.

The staff at Mundo Marino have since become experts in rescuing marine animals from pollution, which deplorably and inexcusably still ravages wildlife the world over. With nearly forty years' involvement in work of this kind, the senior staff are acknowledged globally as authorities in the rehabilitation of animals damaged by environmental disasters and they are ready to respond to calls for assistance wherever and whenever they happen. Since 1987, when record-keeping began, more than 2,500 penguins have been rescued, of which about three-quarters had been the victims of oil pollution.

I was ecstatic to be allowed the privilege of entering the penguin enclosure. Here, under an enormous canopy, perhaps a hundred Magellan penguins were behaving exactly as I remembered them in the wilds of Punta Tombo and I revelled in the moment. Had there been facilities like these in the zoo in Buenos Aires I don't doubt I would have entrusted Juan Salvado into their safekeeping.

I was given a bucket of fish and the opportunity to feed the birds and, of course, I jumped at the chance. It had been so many years since I had last fed a penguin — my penguin — and the lump in my throat was hard to ignore. The fish were significantly larger than the sprats I had bought in the Quilmes market, but, just as I had done for Juan Salvado, I took one by the tail and held it out temptingly for the penguin nearest to me. The bird apparently had no idea what to do and one of the keepers showed me a technique that involved holding the penguin's head in the palm of one's hand while closing thumb and forefinger under its beak. Thus blindfolded, the penguin started snapping for food and took the fish it was given. I was intrigued. This method was so much more cumbersome and time-consuming than the simple and obvious method we had used with Juan Salvado, so I asked how the technique had come about.

It was during the keeper's careful explanation about how newcomers have to be force-fed — just as I had discovered with Juan Salvado — until they got used to feeding in the water that I lost concentration. I suddenly caught sight of a single penguin that stood out among the crowd of monochrome birds. With his extravagant, luxurious eyebrows together with orange eyes and beak, the lone rockhopper penguin found it impossible to be anonymous amid the rest. For no reason obvious to me, this little bird abruptly started making his way through the penguin crowds and directly towards my feet as though he were on an errand of supreme importance.

He hopped up on to a conveniently situated large rock and looked up at me in a beseeching sort of way, which said, 'Will you scratch my tummy, please?' Naturally, I was overjoyed to oblige, so I stooped and gently rubbed his chest. Of course, he felt exactly like Juan Salvado and he responded in exactly the same way, by pressing against my fingers and looking straight into my eyes.

In answer to my enquiry about him, I was told he was the single rockhopper from a group of rescued birds and, although he had now fully recovered, he couldn't be released until another rehabilitated rockhopper was ready to be set at liberty. 'You can't release penguins on their own,' the keeper explained. 'Like sea lions, come to that, they simply won't go without a fellow creature of their own kind; they won't leave.'

What a revelation! Suddenly, after all the years of wondering why Juan Salvado had so persistently refused to leave me on that beach in Punta del Este, I felt I had a satisfactory answer at last. Oh, the relief! It had been less to do with wet feathers and more to do with the fundamental psychology of penguins. A giant smile crept across my face because, finally, I had found some peace of mind; the very last piece of the puzzle had just fallen into place. How strange is coincidence? Had that rockhopper not been there, had our paths not met, I might never have found the final part of the jigsaw. But how sad for him. This particular penguin was stuck there, confined not by the fences but by his own nature and instincts, until some new disaster brought another injured or polluted rockhopper to Mundo Marino.

Now, ever since the days of my compadre, Juan Salvado, I have steadfastly believed Magellan penguins to be quite the most handsome and distinguished of all the biological order *Spheniscidae*, while rockhoppers — with their spiky hairdos, foolish, ostentatious and theatrical 'fascinators' — were the representatives of the disreputable, bohemian, punk side of the family. However, stroking that little bird, I discovered, as all too often before I'm afraid, that my prejudices were founded on nothing more substantial than appearances. As the little rockhopper penguin pushed back against my hand, he studied me, first with one eye and then the other, just like Juan Salvado used to do. Just as intently, I observed him in turn, with his feathered feet, exquisite plumage and eyes that were limpid amber pools of unfathomable depth. I was utterly enthralled by this beautiful and enchanting creature.

And at that moment I knew for certain, beyond the slightest shadow of a doubt, that given a fair wind, a string bag and half a chance, I would unhesitatingly have set out on a South American adventure once again — with a penguin!

Glossary of Spanish terms

aguinaldo bonus
aliscafo hydrofoil
asado barbecue
bajo the area by the river, low-lying
basta enough
bombachas cowboy trousers
brasileños cattle rustlers
campo farmed land
colectivo bus
compañeros comrades
Cumpleaños Feliz 'Happy Birthday' in Spanish.
  If you were wishing someone a happy birthday
  you would say *'Feliz Cumpleaños'*, but if you
  sing 'Happy Birthday' it is *'Cumpleaños Feliz'*.
descamisados 'shirtless ones', labourers
facón gaucho knife
hielo ice
hola hello
Madre de Dios Mother of God
magnífico magnificent, wonderful
mate Argentine tea
mestizo mixed race, usually a mix of European
  and American Indian ancestry
momentito just a second
mozo waiter
muchísimas gracias thank you very much
ñandú South American ostrich, rhea
paleta Argentine version of squash
quebracho a type of hard wood

¿Qué tal? How's things?
salud cheers
subte subway
subterráneo underground

Acknowledgements

I owe a debt of gratitude to many people for all their support, encouragement and assistance in telling the story of Juan Salvador the penguin. To Jessica Leeke of Penguin Random House who ceaselessly championed the cause, to Laura Warner who 'found' us and to Karen Whitlock, my copyeditor. I am greatly appreciative of everything that these skilled and dedicated professionals have done. To Mike Tate, formerly of *The Times*, a man of letters and stalwart friend. To my mother, who so carefully archived all the things I sent home, but most of all to my wonderful wife and children, without whom I would never have picked up my pen. Thank you.

Other titles published by Ulverscroft:

PRIVATE VIEW

Alexandra Connor

Behind universally admired works of art — *The Laughing Cavalier* by Hals, *The Birth of Venus* by Botticelli, *The Thinker* by Rodin, and many more — are the artists themselves, whose lesser-known eccentricities are revealed in *Private View*. Here is Fra Filippo Lippi, a friar who had to be locked in a room by the Pope in order to keep him at the easel and away from the bedroom. William Blake, who talked to the dead — and Theodore Gericault, who brought the dead home with him to use as unpaid models. Here is Rembrandt, who not only owned a monkey himself, but once painted a similar creature into a patron's family portrait. And of course the swaggering Michelangelo, who as a child recommended his 'perfect' services 'in all humility' to the Duke of Milan . . .

GOODBYE EAST END

David Merron

As Hitler's bombs threatened London during the Second World War, eight-year-old David Merron was evacuated from his family and the close-knit Jewish community in the East End to the safety of the English countryside. Placed in the care of strangers, this new life was sometimes unpredictable and lonely. But, with time, the great outdoors became an exciting adventure playground in which he flourished. Set against a dramatic wartime backdrop, this is the story of a conflict between a boy's unexpected love of the countryside and his guilt about not missing home as much as he might, and of the childhood experiences that changed his life forever.

AS GREEN AS GRASS

Emma Smith

Uprooted from her beloved Great Western Beach, Emma Smith and her family move from Newquay to the Devonshire village of Crapstone. Tragedy strikes when Emma's father suffers a catastrophic breakdown and, in 1939, war becomes a reality. Determined to make a difference to the war effort, Emma chooses to work on canal boats, where she must learn to deal with hard manual labour, a sinking vessel, and buckets instead of toilets. When the war finally ends, Emma's new-found adventurous spirit takes her all over the world: to literary London, where she meets Laurie Lee; to India to film a love story; to France, where she falls helplessly in love. This is the story of an unusual woman determined, against a backdrop of enormous social change, to be a writer, come what may.